CHOOSING NOT TO CHOOSE

CHOOSING NOT TO CHOOSE

Understanding the Value of Choice

Cass R. Sunstein

OXFORD
UNIVERSITY PRESS

OXFORD
UNIVERSITY PRESS

Oxford University Press is a department of the University of Oxford. It furthers the University's objective of excellence in research, scholarship, and education by publishing worldwide.

Oxford   New York

Auckland   Cape Town   Dar es Salaam   Hong Kong   Karachi   Kuala Lumpur   Madrid
Melbourne   Mexico City   Nairobi   New Delhi   Shanghai   Taipei   Toronto

With offices in

Argentina   Austria   Brazil   Chile   Czech Republic   France   Greece   Guatemala   Hungary
Italy   Japan   Poland   Portugal   Singapore   South Korea   Switzerland   Thailand
Turkey   Ukraine   Vietnam

Oxford is a registered trademark of Oxford University Press in the UK and certain other countries.

Published in the United States of America by
Oxford University Press
198 Madison Avenue, New York, NY 10016

Library of Congress Cataloging-in-Publication Data
Sunstein, Cass R.
Choosing not to choose : understanding the value of choice / Cass R. Sunstein.
   pages cm
Includes bibliographical references and index.
ISBN 978-0-19-023169-9 (hardback)
1. Choice (Psychology) 2. Decision making. I. Title.
BF611.S87 2015
53.8'3—dc23
                                                                                    2014035565

1 3 5 7 9 8 6 4 2

Printed in the United States of America on acid-free paper

Note to Readers

To the memory of Edna Ullmann-Margalit

There are these two young fish swimming along and they happen to meet an older fish swimming the other way, who nods at them and says "Morning, boys. How's the water?" And the two young fish swim on for a bit, and then eventually one of them looks over at the other and goes "What the hell is water?"

David Foster Wallace

"But I don't want comfort. I want God, I want poetry, I want real danger, I want freedom, I want goodness. I want sin."

"In fact," said Mustapha Mond, "you're claiming the right to be unhappy."

"All right then," said the Savage defiantly, "I'm claiming the right to be unhappy."

"Not to mention the right to grow old and ugly and impotent; the right to have syphilis and cancer; the right to have too little to eat; the right to be lousy; the right to live in constant apprehension of what may happen to-morrow; the right to catch typhoid; the right to be tortured by unspeakable pains of every kind."

There was a long silence.

"I claim them all," said the Savage at last.

Aldous Huxley, Brave New World

CONTENTS

CONTENTS

PART THREE
THE FUTURE

PREFACE

Choice is often an extraordinary benefit, a kind of blessing, but it can also be an immense burden, a kind of curse. Time and attention are precious commodities, and we cannot focus on everything, even when our interests and our values are at stake. If we had to make choices about everything that affects us, we would be overwhelmed. Learning can be costly, and it isn't always fun. Sometimes we exercise our freedom, and we improve our welfare, by choosing not to choose. That choice opens up time and space for us, enabling us to focus on our real concerns. Establishing these claims, and identifying their limitations, are the purposes of this book.

It is true that much of the time, human beings like to choose. Freedom-loving societies respect that desire. You don't own sneakers, cell phones, books, or automobiles unless you have selected them. Moreover, much of your choosing is active rather than passive. To get something, you have to express your wishes. Companies aren't allowed to presume that you want to buy a new electric car or a home near the beach, or a subscription to a magazine focusing on teenage musicians. You must explicitly express your will. That is an important part of freedom. In the political and social domains, the same points certainly hold. No one presumes how you want to vote, or defaults you into supporting the incumbent. And in free societies, you choose your religion, your political convictions, and your spouse.

In nations that respect liberty, two things seem to be true. The first is that you get to choose. The second is that you have to choose.

All this is so, partly, and we will explore in detail why this is so, but we will also investigate the other side of the story. One way that people display their agency is by choosing not to choose. People might do that explicitly, delegating certain powers to their governments, their employers, their advisers, their friends, or their spouses. When you use a GPS, you are effectively asking it to choose a route for you; it provides a default route, which you can ignore if you like. Or people may make a delegation implicitly; everyone may know that they don't want to make certain choices. We often think, or even say (sometimes with enthusiasm, sometimes with irritation), "You decide." In some situations, that particular choice makes us a lot better off.

When websites ask you to check a box saying "Don't ask me again," a lot of people are happy to check that box. If public officials, or doctors, ask you to fill out numerous and duplicative forms, registering choices of multiple kinds, you may get immensely frustrated and wish that at least some of those choices had been made for you. (People would be better off if public and private institutions cut existing form-filling requirements dramatically.) And if a cab driver insists on asking you to choose which route you want to take in an unfamiliar city, you might wish he hadn't asked, and just selected the route that he deems best. (When you are having lunch or dinner with a friend, it's often most considerate to suggest a place, rather than asking the friend to choose.)

There is a related point. Our lives are actually full of things that we have by default, and without necessarily exercising our power to choose. *Deciding by default* is an omnipresent (and often wonderful) feature of human life. You may have chosen a cell phone, but you didn't choose all of its features, and it has a lot of default settings, many of which you can change if you wish. If you decide to work for a particular employer, you might well find yourself with a health insurance plan, a retirement plan, and a series of rights and obligations that you did not specifically select (though you might well be able to change them). If you are a student, default rules establish much of your relationship with your college or university. Countless decisions are made by default, in the sense that some kind of presumption or default rule is in place, subject to override by those who are affected.

There is a close connection between these points and the question of wealth and poverty. If you are wealthy, and live in a wealthy or well-functioning nation, you are free by default, in the sense that the social background is just fine, and you don't have to devote your time and attention to making it so. If you are poor, or live in a poor or dysfunctional country, your freedom is badly compromised, in the sense that the social background is far from fine, and it forces you to attend to a large number of problems that rich people, or people in rich or well-functioning nations, need not worry over. You are unfree by default. You are not in chains, at least not literally, but life might start to feel that way. There is a high cost to being poor, and one of those costs is cognitive. The sheer number of questions to which you must attend, and the difficulty of managing your life, reduce or maybe even obliterate your ability to attend to matters that most interest and concern you, perhaps including your own personal and professional development. If you lack time, you lack freedom. It is no accident that people who are in jail are said to be "serving time."

These claims are meant as essentially timeless and universal truths. They are about the human condition. But there is a more immediate point, and it is distinctive to our era. The world is now in the midst of a period of extraordinary technological change, in which the nature of default rules, and the relationship between choices and defaults, is very much in flux. More than at any time in human history, it is simple to ask people: *What, exactly, do you want?* Active choosing is feasible in countless areas, whether the question involves health care, travel preferences, investments, or computer settings. Where people used to have to rely on others, or to defer to some kind of default, they can now decide on their own.

There is a sharply contrasting development, and it is also occurring in the current era. More than at any point in human history, it is feasible to tailor defaults to people's personal situations. If you are young or old, male or female, tall or small, fat or thin, rich or poor, well-educated or not, a default can be selected for you. Indeed, it is feasible to go much further. If you are John Smith or Mary Williams, a default can be chosen *just for you*—on the basis of what is known about you, and perhaps even on the basis of a comprehensive understanding, or profile, of your own previous choices. Once you have made a large number of choices, and perhaps once you have made just one or a few, you might find yourself with a series of *personalized default rules*, covering a lot of your life. We can even imagine a system of *predictive shopping*, through which people enroll in programs, or are enrolled in programs, by which they receive goods and services, and are billed for them, on the basis of an algorithm predicting what they need and like.

That might sound like science fiction, but it's on the way. With the help of large data sets ("big data"), it is increasingly easy for providers to know what you, or people like you, tend to like. Many providers now offer a high degree of automaticity. Any particular list will soon become dated, but consider a few examples. If you find shoes that you like, JackRabbit sports will send you a new pair of your preferred sneakers every four to six months. If you are male and like particular brands of socks, deodorants, underwear, or condoms, Manpacks.com will send them to you every three months or so. Petco Repeat Delivery allows you to order an initial delivery of pet food, and thereafter you will receive deliveries when and as you need them (with a confirmatory email enabling you to cancel if you wish).

In these cases, and many others, you can choose once, and choose not to choose thereafter. (Recall the magical words "Don't ask me again.") And in some domains, it may not be necessary for you to choose at all. In a recent period, American homeowners lost over $5 billion because of a failure to refinance their homes. Apparently the act of applying, and making a few simple choices, has been too daunting.[1] A system with automatic refinancing, when it turned out to be in people's interests, would save homeowners a lot of money. Such a system could be highly personalized, with refinancing deals designed to fit people's particular situations.

Is the rise of personalized default rules a blessing or a curse? Short answer: Blessing. Is it a utopian or dystopian vision? Short answer: Utopian. But no short answer is sufficient. This book offers a framework with which to answer these questions. I am going to celebrate default rules (mostly), and remark on their contribution to human freedom, and we will explore why people choose not to choose, but we will also have a lot to say in favor of active choosing. We will investigate the particular advantages of *simplified active choosing*, by which people are asked whether they want to make a choice—or instead to rely on a default. I will spend some time examining whether active choices or default rules are best, and when, and why.

---

1. *See* Benjamin Keys et al., *Failure to Refinance* (2014), *available at* http://www.nber.org/papers/w20401.pdf.

CHOOSING NOT TO CHOOSE

INTRODUCTION

Choices

Consider the following problems:

1. Public officials are deciding whether to require people, as a condition for obtaining a driver's license, to make an active choice about whether they want to become organ donors. The alternatives are to continue with the existing "opt-in" system, in which people become organ donors only if they affirmatively indicate their consent, or to change to an "opt-out" system, in which consent is presumed.[1]

2. A private company is deciding among three options: to enroll employees automatically in a health insurance plan; to ask them to opt in if they like; or to say that as a condition for starting work, they must indicate whether they want health insurance, and if so, which plan they want.

3. A utility company is deciding whether to adopt for consumers a "green default," with a somewhat more expensive but

---

1. We could also imagine situations in which people are effectively prompted to choose, by being explicitly asked whether they would like to do so, without in any sense being required to choose. For an interesting empirical result, see Judd Kessler & Alvin Roth, *Don't Take "No" for an Answer: An Experiment with Actual Organ Donor Registrations* (2014), *available at* http://www.nber.org/papers/w20378 (finding that required active choosing has a smaller effect, in terms of getting people to sign up for organ donation, than prompted choice).

environmentally preferable energy source, or instead a "gray default," with a somewhat less expensive but environmentally less desirable energy source, or alternatively to ask consumers which energy source they prefer.

4. A social networking site is deciding whether to adopt a system of default settings for privacy, or whether to require first-time users to say, as a condition for access to the site, what privacy settings they would prefer.

5. A state is contemplating a method of making voting more automatic, by allowing people to visit a website at any time to indicate that they want to vote for all candidates from one or another party and even to say, if they wish, that they would like to continue voting for such candidates in future elections until they explicitly indicate otherwise.

6. An online bookseller has compiled a great deal of information about the choices of its customers, and in some cases it believes that it knows what people want before they know themselves. It is contemplating a system of "predictive shopping." With that system it would send people certain books, and charge their credit card for those books, before they make their wishes known. The company is also considering whether to ask people to make an active choice to enroll in a system of predictive shopping or instead to enroll them automatically. (In chapter 7, I will present some evidence on how Americans think about this possibility; the answers may surprise you.)

In all of these cases, an institution is deciding whether to use some kind of default rule or instead to require some kind of active choice. (I shall say a good deal about what the word "require" might mean in this setting.) For those who reject paternalism and who prize freedom of choice, active choosing has evident appeal. Indeed it might seem far preferable to any kind of default rule.

Those who decide between active choosing and default rules are *choice architects*, in the sense that they design the social context within which choices are made.[2] The idea of "social context" should be understood very broadly. It includes temperature, colors, sizes, shapes, and sounds. (If candy is wrapped in a green package, health-conscious consumers are more likely to buy it, whether or not it is actually healthy.) It includes the order in which options are presented and in which people's attention is triggered. (If an item is first on a list, it's more likely to be chosen, and the same is true if it is listed last; items listed in the middle don't get a lot of attention.) It emphatically includes default rules—and it includes active choosing as well. Choice architecture specifies when, whether, and how we choose. Whether or not people are aware of it, choice architecture is everywhere. It is not possible to dispense with a social context, and some kind of choice architecture is therefore inevitable.

In that sense, it is pointless to wish it away. Writers might as well wish away the existence of language. The analogy is close, because choice architecture enables and facilitates at the same time that it constrains and limits. Recall my first epigraph here, from a 2005 commencement speech by the great novelist David Foster Wallace:[3]

There are these two young fish swimming along and they happen to meet an older fish swimming the other way, who nods at them and says "Morning, boys. How's the water?" And the two young fish swim on for a bit, and then eventually one of them looks over at the other and goes "What the hell is water?"

2. RICHARD H. THALER & CASS R. SUNSTEIN, NUDGE: IMPROVING DECISIONS ABOUT HEALTH, WEALTH, AND HAPPINESS 3 (2008).
3. *Available at* http://moreintelligentlife.com/story/david-foster-wallace-in-his-own-words.

As water is to the young fish, choice architecture is to human beings. People may not notice it, but it's nonetheless there. Moreover, default rules, even or perhaps especially if they are taken for granted, count as prime "nudges," understood as interventions that maintain freedom of choice, that do not impose mandates or bans, but that nonetheless incline people's choices in a particular direction.[4] A GPS, which enables people to choose not to choose, is another example of a nudge; a disclosure requirement falls in the same category. Default rules can be effective nudges, and they are (I think) the most interesting of all.

When private or public institutions establish a default rule, they may be counting on people's reluctance to choose, but they do not force anyone to do anything. On the contrary, they maintain freedom of choice. Whether people must opt out or opt in, they are permitted to do so as they see fit.[5] What is striking and immensely important is that default rules nonetheless have a large impact, because they tend to stick.

If a private or public institution seeks to alter outcomes, switching the default rule may be a highly effective route—perhaps more effective than significant economic incentives (as in the case of retirement savings). Of course such incentives matter. If you increase the price of something, people will usually buy less of it. But sometimes people ignore incentives, especially if they have other things on which to focus.[6] People sometimes ignore default

---

4. See Thaler & Sunstein, *supra* note 2, at 6; *see also* Stefano DellaVigna & Ulrike Malmendier, *Paying Not to Go to the Gym*, 96 Am. Econ. Rev. 694, 716 (2006) (exploring an illuminating example of how default rules can be used in the domain of exercise).

5. *But see* Riccardo Rebonato, Taking Liberties 83–86 (2012) (arguing that some choice-preserving measures lack easy reversibility and resemble forms of hard paternalism); *see also* Cass R. Sunstein, *The Storrs Lectures: Behavioral Economics and Paternalism*, 122 Yale L.J. 1826, 1893–94.

6. *Cf.* Andrew Caplin & Daniel J. Martin, *Defaults and Attention: The Drop Out Effect* 16–19 (Nat'l Bureau of Econ. Research, Working Paper No. 17988, 2012), *available at* http://

rules, too, but for choice architects that is an opportunity, not a problem. Default rules can stick when and because people ignore them. Here, then, is a striking difference between incentives and default rules. Incentives will have an effect only when and because people attend to them. Default rules can have an effect when and because people pay no attention to them.

It follows that with respect to health care, romance, marriage, financial markets, consumer protection, poverty, the availability of organs, energy use, environmental protection, obesity, mortgages, savings, and much more, the choice of the default rule is exceedingly important. Public-spirited or self-interested people in both the private and public spheres can and do use choice architecture, including default rules, to produce outcomes they deem desirable.

LIFE AND LAW

One of the most important tasks of a legal system is to establish default rules. Indeed, many important policies operate through default rules, often in the form of presumptions, and contract law consists in large part of such rules.[7] What happens if the parties are silent on whether employees may be fired only "for cause," or instead for whatever reason the employer deems fit? A default rule might specify the answer, and it might well stick.[8] If the legal system

---

www.nber.org/papers/w17988 (positing that informative defaults lead people to "drop out" and pay less attention to the choices they make).

7. *See* Ian Ayres & Robert Gertner, *Filling Gaps in Incomplete Contracts: An Economic Theory of Default Rules*, 99 YALE L.J. 87 (1989). For an important discussion of presumptions in law and elsewhere, with many implications, see Edna Ullmann-Margalit, *On Presumption*, 80 J. PHIL. 143 (1983).

8. *See* Russell Korobkin, *The Status Quo Bias and Contract Default Rules*, 83 CORNELL L. REV. 608, 625–30 (1998) (discussing how preexisting defaults alter personal preferences); *see also* Samuel Issacharoff, *Contracting for Employment: The Limited*

creates such a rule, contracting parties might not reject it even if they can do so pretty easily. Sometimes they say, "yeah, whatever"— and the default rule sticks.

Of course, many legal rules are mandatory; they do not merely set the default. You cannot opt out of the prohibition on murder or assault. If power plants are emitting unlawfully high levels of pollution, they face penalties; they cannot opt out. Employers cannot ask employees to opt out of the prohibition on racial discrimination or sexual harassment. But even in the most sensitive and controversial contexts, default rules are in place, and they are exceedingly important.

Consider, for example, the problem of age discrimination. The United States allows people to waive their antidiscrimination right at the point of retirement, subject to certain constraints.[9] The basic idea is that older workers should have a right not to face discrimination—but that they should be allowed to "trade" their right to sue in return for a suitable retirement package. People are often allowed to waive their right to a jury trial or even their right to bring suit at all. Plea bargains are themselves a form of waiver. In the criminal justice system, people have many rights by default, but they can give them up if they choose. If people can choose to waive their rights, don't they have more liberty? At least if the choice is both real and informed, and not a charade? At least most of the time?

Here is another legal analogue. People often hire agents. You can hire someone to make financial decisions for you, and you can give people "power of attorney," enabling them to make a wide range

Return of the Common Law, 74 Tex. L. Rev. 1783, 1789–90 (1996) (discussing how the common law intervened when parties failed to specify the bases on which an employer could terminate the employer–employee relationship).

9. 29 U.S.C. § 626(f)(1) (2006). Note that the right is waivable for past violations, but not for future violations.

of important choices on your behalf. In both formal and informal ways, people act as "principals," hiring agents to execute their wishes. The president of the United States has a number of agents, including his cabinet, and the head of a large corporation is surrounded by agents who work for her. A complex body of law—"principal-agent law"—governs the precise relationships between principals and agents. For present purposes, the crucial point is that for many matters, principals choose not to choose. Indeed, that is the central point of the principal–agent relationship. It is true that the agent owes a duty of loyalty to the principal, that the agent's discretion may be sharply bounded, that the principal is ultimately in charge, and that there are a number of choices that an agent cannot make and a number of factors that an agent cannot consider. But whenever principals hire agents, it is because they choose not to choose, at least across a certain terrain. Often that choice is indispensable, in the sense that it frees up the principal to focus on the most important topics—and also in the sense that it ensures that decisions will be made by people who really know what they are doing.

ON LIBERTY

All of the approaches that I will be exploring here are meant to preserve freedom. A default rule allows people to choose to choose—and also to choose not to choose (by relying on the default). There is much to be said for that choice. A humble example: Your employer might default you into a pension plan and inform you that you do not have to bother about it—but if you don't like the plan, you can change it.

True, some people do not much like defaults, and they much prefer active choosing. I will have a great deal to say about that preference. But a natural question arises from the view, widely supported in the liberal political tradition, that government legitimately interferes with private choices only to prevent "harm to others." In a famous passage in his essay *On Liberty*, John Stuart Mill insisted:

> The only purpose for which power can be rightfully exercised over any member of a civilized community, against his will, is to prevent harm to others. His own good, either physical or moral, is not a sufficient warrant. He cannot rightfully be compelled to do or forbear because it will be better for him to do so, because it will make him happier, because, in the opinion of others, to do so would be wise, or even right.[10]

This passage raises many questions of interpretation. But Mill's argument must reckon with the fact that public institutions, no less than private ones, establish default rules, and these represent an exercise of power. Mill did not discuss default rules, and perhaps such rules can be squared with his basic account; I believe so. Certainly such rules do not "compel" anyone to do or to forbear. But choice architects often select default rules on the ground that they help to produce decisions that will make people happier or otherwise better off, and that are either wise or right. Whether this justification is a point against such rules and in favor of active choosing requires careful consideration, not any kind of slogan.

Mill offered a number of separate arguments for his famous harm principle, but one of his most important, and the most relevant here, is that individuals are in the best position to know what is good for them. In Mill's view, the problem with outsiders, including government officials, is that they lack the necessary information.

10. JOHN STUART MILL, ON LIBERTY (2d ed. 1863), *reprinted in* THE BASIC WRITINGS OF JOHN STUART MILL: ON LIBERTY, THE SUBJECTION OF WOMEN, AND UTILITARIANISM 3, 11–12 (Dale E. Miller ed., 2002).

Mill insists that the individual "is the person most interested in his own well-being" and the "ordinary man or woman has means of knowledge immeasurably surpassing those that can be possessed by anyone else." When society seeks to overrule the individual's judgment, it does so on the basis of "general presumptions," and these "may be altogether wrong, and even if right are as likely as not to be misapplied to individual cases." If the goal is to ensure that people's lives go well, Mill contends that the best solution is for public officials to allow people to find their own paths.

No one should deny that Mill's claim has a great deal of intuitive appeal. But is it correct? That is largely an empirical question, and it cannot be adequately answered by introspection and intuition. In recent decades, some of the most important research in social science, coming from psychologists and behavioral economists, has been trying to answer it. That research is having a significant influence on public officials throughout the world. Behavioral findings are raising questions about some of the foundations of Mill's argument, because they establish that people make a lot of mistakes about their own well-being and that those mistakes can prove extremely damaging.[11]

Within recent social science, authoritatively discussed by Daniel Kahneman in his masterful *Thinking, Fast and Slow*, it has become standard to suggest that the human mind contains not one but two "cognitive systems."[12] In the social science literature, the two systems are unimaginatively described as System 1 and System 2. System 1 is the automatic system, while System 2 is more deliberative and reflective.

---

11. DANIEL KAHNEMAN, THINKING, FAST AND SLOW (2011). On behavioral economics and public policy in general, see CASS R. SUNSTEIN, SIMPLER: THE FUTURE OF GOVERNMENT (2013); THALER & SUNSTEIN, *supra* note 2.

12. KAHNEMAN, *supra* note 11.

System 1 works fast. Much of the time, it is on automatic pilot. It is driven by habits. It can be emotional and intuitive. When it hears a loud noise, it is inclined to run. When it is offended, it wants to hit back. It certainly eats a delicious brownie. It can procrastinate; it can be impulsive. It can also "precrastinate," that is, engage in a series of tasks too early, in a way that results in serious and unnecessary burdens and costs.[13] It can be excessively fearful, and too complacent. It wants what it wants when it wants it. It is a doer, not a planner. System 1 is a bit like Homer Simpson, James Dean (in *Rebel without a Cause*), and Pippi Longstocking.

System 2 is more like a computer or Mr. Spock in *Star Trek*. It is deliberative. It calculates. It hears a loud noise, and it assesses whether the noise is a cause for concern. It thinks about probability, carefully though sometimes slowly. It does not really get offended. If it sees reasons for offense, it makes a careful assessment of what, all things considered, ought to be done. It sees a delicious brownie, and it makes a judgment about whether, all things considered, it should eat it. It insists on the importance of self-control. It is a planner more than a doer.

In human life, System 1 often runs the show. People can be myopic and impulsive, giving undue weight to the short term (perhaps by smoking, perhaps by texting while driving, perhaps by eating too much chocolate).[14] What is *salient* (in the sense of "cognitively accessible") greatly matters.[15] If an important feature of a situation, an activity, or a product does not readily come to mind, people might ignore it, possibly to their advantage (perhaps because it is in the other room,

---

13. David A. Rosenbaum et al., *Pre-Crastination: Hastening Subgoal Completion at the Expense of Extra Physical Effort*, 25 PSYCHOL. SCI. 1487 (2014).

14. *See* David Laibson, *Golden Eggs and Hyperbolic Discounting*, 112 Q.J. ECON. 443, 445 (1997).

15. For a discussion of some of the foundational issues, see Pedro Bordalo, Nicola Gennaioli, & Andrei Shleifer, *Salience Theory of Choice Under Risk*, 127 Q.J. ECON. 1243 (2012); Pedro Bordalo, Nicola Gennaioli, & Andrei Shleifer, *Salience in Experimental Tests of the Endowment Effect*, 102 AM. ECON. REV. 47 (2012).

and fattening) and possibly to their detriment (if it could save them money or extend their lives).

People procrastinate and sometimes suffer as a result; recall the failure to refinance.[16] They can be unrealistically optimistic and for that reason make unfortunate and even dangerous choices.[17] People make "affective forecasting errors": they predict that activities or products will have certain beneficial or adverse effects on their own well-being, but those predictions turn out to be wrong, sometimes grievously so.[18]

In these circumstances, sensible default rules can provide a lot of help. Knowing that we focus on the short term, that we suffer from inertia, that we fail to plan, and that we might fall victim to unrealistic optimism, we select default rules—or applaud those who select such rules for us. Human beings make a lot of "second-order decisions"—decisions about decisions—and choosing not to choose is an important one of them.[19] We want to strengthen the hand of System 2. One way of doing so is by choosing not to choose.

A small example: Many people set up a system of automatic payment for their credit card bills, thus making it unnecessary for them to think, every month, about when and how to pay. They ensure that full payment is the default. They do the same thing for a range of other payments—for club membership, for charitable giving,

---

16. See Ted O'Donoghue & Matthew Rabin, *Choice and Procrastination*, 116 Q.J. Econ. 121, 121–22 (2001); Richard H. Thaler & Shlomo Benartzi, *Save More Tomorrow™: Using Behavioral Economics to Increase Employee Saving*, 112 J. Pol. Econ. S164, S168–69 (2004).

17. See Tali Sharot, The Optimism Bias: A Tour of the Irrationally Positive Brain (2011).

18. See, e.g., Elizabeth W. Dunn, Daniel T. Gilbert, & Timothy D. Wilson, *If Money Doesn't Make You Happy, Then You Probably Aren't Spending It Right*, 21 J. Consumer Psychol. 115 (2011); Daniel T. Gilbert et al., *Immune Neglect: A Source of Durability Bias in Affective Forecasting*, 75 J. Personality & Soc. Psychol. 617 (1998).

19. Cass R. Sunstein & Edna Ullmann-Margalit, *Second-Order Decisions*, 110 Ethics 5 (1999).

for the salaries of employees. Default rules often enlist automaticity in order to help overcome various behavioral biases and also to respond to the fact that human beings inevitably have limited "bandwidth."[20] (This is not only an example but also a hint: People's lives can go much better if they make bill-paying and other things automatic, and hence do not have to worry about them. One choice can establish a process that makes it unnecessary for people to choose in the future.)

But if human beings are genuinely prone to error, it might well be argued that default rules are not enough—that mandates and bans are necessary to protect people against their own mistakes. In some circumstances, this argument is right. In many free societies, people cannot buy certain medicines without a prescription—a clear case of paternalism. Occupational safety and health laws prevent workers from running some risks that they would readily agree to run. Whatever Mill might have thought, paternalistic interferences with freedom of choice are hardly absent from nations that generally respect liberty, and the risk of human error helps to explain when such interferences are justified.

At the same time, it is no light thing to eliminate freedom of choice. Default rules have the important virtue of providing a safety valve in the face of errors or bad motivations on the part of choice architects. I shall have a fair bit to say about this issue in chapter 8.

FOUR GOALS

In this book I have four goals. The first and most general is to demonstrate that sensible default rules, making it unnecessary for us to

---

20. *See* SENDHIL MULLAINATHAN & ELDAR SHAFIR, SCARCITY (2013).

choose, help to make our lives both better and more free. Default rules are inevitable, and human beings cannot possibly do without them. If we eliminated them, we would quickly be overburdened, even overwhelmed.[21] If the point is not obvious, it is only because default rules are frequently invisible. Even when they have a large effect, and even when they make our daily lives simpler and even possible, we may not notice them. Indeed, that might be the point. My second goal is to see when default rules matter and when they do not, and exactly why. Inertia is a powerful force, and it can lead people to stick with the default rule, even if they do not exactly love it. Busy people might not want to focus on changing the default, even if it is easy for them to do so. Default rules also convey information; you might conclude that sensible people, or experts, selected them for a good reason. If choice architects select one default rather than another, people might think that their choice is probably best. (Some universities, including my own, choose a retirement plan for faculty members, operating as a kind of default that professors can reject; like many people, I assume that my university knows what it is doing.) In some cases, people's preferences do not antedate the default rule or stand apart from it. We do not know, exactly, what we want, and the default rule plays a role in creating our preferences, values, and desires.[22] In such cases, default rules have a lot of power.

---

21. *See, e.g.,* Anuj K. Shah et al., *Some Consequences of Having Too Little,* 338 SCIENCE 682, 682 (2012) (addressing the competition for an individual's attention and its impact on decisionmaking). Barry Schwartz's highly illuminating book THE PARADOX OF CHOICE (2007) explores the problem of "choice overload" in great detail and contends that it is often better for people to have fewer choices than more. While my topic is different, it is closely related, as will be evident, I have learned a great deal from Schwartz's exploration of the various problems associated with excessive choice.

22. *See* Eric J. Johnson & Daniel G. Goldstein, *Decisions by Default, in* THE BEHAVIORAL FOUNDATIONS OF POLICY 417, 425 (Eldar Shafir ed., 2013) (discussing how default rules might overcome organ shortages and encourage donation).

It is for this reason, among others, that default rules serve as a highly attractive alternative to incentives as a means of altering outcomes—potentially less expensive and more effective.[23] Because default rules specify a particular outcome in the (often likely) event of inaction, they can have a much larger effect than significant economic incentives. From the standpoint of standard economic thinking, that is a big surprise. In principle, default rules, which people can easily reject, should not be as effective as economic incentives. On this count, however, standard economic thinking is sometimes wrong. Choice architects may well be able to use default rules to produce outcomes that could otherwise be achieved only through substantial expenditures of resources. Indeed, both private and public institutions are already doing exactly that.

My third goal is to specify the appropriate place of *active choosing*, and in the process to explore why and when people want to choose, or instead choose not to choose. Many people are, of course, suspicious of default rules and see them as a form of manipulation or subterfuge. They want people to choose instead. In some contexts, they are entirely right. A great deal of the discussion here will try to explain why this is so—and thus justify the common intuition that people should choose to choose.

My fourth and final goal is to explore the uses and limits of personalized default rules. Such rules attempt to distinguish among

---

23. *Id.* One study finds that a default rule has a far greater effect than significant economic incentives in promoting savings, as reflected in the authors' suggestion: "[A]utomatic contributions are more effective at increasing savings rates than price subsidies for three reasons: (1) subsidies induce relatively few individuals to respond, (2) they generate substantial crowdout condition on response, and (3) they do not *influence* the savings behavior of passive individuals, who are at least prepared for retirement." Raj Chetty et al., *Active vs. Passive Decisions and Crowdout in Retirement Savings Accounts: Evidence from Denmark* 1 (Nat'l Bureau of Econ. Research, Working Paper No. 13-01, 2012), *available at* http://www.nber.org/aging/rrc/papers/orrc13-01.pdf.

members of the relevant population, ensuring (in the extreme case) that each individual receives a default rule that fits his or her particular situation. With a personalized default, you are given an outcome that makes best sense for you.

The great promise of personalized default rules is that they might eliminate the problems associated with impersonal ones, and do so without imposing the burdens, costs, and potential mistakes of active choosing. As default rules become more personalized, the comparative advantages of active choosing start to diminish. The reason is that personalized approaches can handle the problem of diversity without requiring people to act at all. In many areas, personalized default rules promise to confer large social benefits.

At the same time, personalized default rules create problems of their own. For one thing, they do not promote learning. Choice-making can be seen as a muscle, and it can be good to exercise it and to make it stronger. Personalized defaults may also serve to narrow rather than broaden people's horizons, by promoting outcomes that are consistent with their past choices. In addition, it can be burdensome and expensive for choice architects to produce accurate personalized default rules. Such rules might be used opportunistically by those who are motivated by their own self-interest rather than the interests of potential choosers.

Personalized default rules might also create serious risks to personal privacy. Would you really want choice architects to know enough about you to design default rules that fit your particular situation? It is tempting to answer no, and that answer might well be right—but beware of a simple answer. The privacy issue matters, but it is soluble, perhaps through personalized default rules with respect to privacy itself (more later on that). We will also see that even if they are personalized, default rules do not provide what active choosing does: a sense of personal responsibility and of close identification with outcomes.

CENTRAL CONCLUSIONS: A PREVIEW

The choice among impersonal default rules, active choosing, and personalized default rules cannot be made in the abstract. To know which is best, both choosers and choice architects need to investigate two factors: the costs of decisions and the costs of errors (understood as the number and magnitude of mistakes). An understanding of those kinds of costs does not tell us everything that we need to know, but it does help to orient the proper analysis of a wide range of problems.

It should be obvious that a default rule can much reduce the costs of decisions. When such a rule is in place, people do not need to focus on what to do; they can simply follow the default. But a default rule can also increase the costs of errors, at least if it does not fit people's situations; it can lead them in directions that make their lives go worse. In approaching the underlying issues, five propositions are clear.

First, impersonal default rules should generally be preferred to active choosing when (1) the context is confusing, technical, and unfamiliar, (2) people would prefer not to choose, (3) learning is not important, and (4) the population is not heterogeneous along any relevant dimension. In cases of this kind, impersonal default rules are a blessing; these are the canonical situations in which such rules make sense. Hard cases can arise when some, but not all, of the four conditions are met. In such cases, an analysis of the costs of decisions and the costs of errors provides helpful orientation but may not produce immediate answers. And even when all four conditions are met, we need to be able to trust choice architects to produce sensible default rules. If those rules are harmful or dumb, it would be best to insist on active choosing.

Second, active choosing should generally be preferred to impersonal default rules when (1) choice architects are biased or lack important information, (2) the context is familiar or nontechnical, (3) people would actually prefer to choose (and hence choice is a benefit rather than a cost), (4) learning matters, and (5) there is relevant heterogeneity. To favor active choosing, it is not necessary that all five conditions be met. The fact that the context is unfamiliar argues against active choosing, because unfamiliarity increases both the costs of decisions and the costs of errors. But even in unfamiliar contexts, there might be a strong argument for active choosing if learning is important or if choice architects are biased. When any one of the five conditions is met, the argument for active choosing is strengthened, but the other conditions might argue in favor of impersonal default rules. We can imagine, for example, cases in which learning would be valuable, but people really do not want to choose, and choice architects can be trusted. To know how to handle such cases, choice architects need to know more about the particular context.

Third, personalized default rules should generally be preferred to impersonal ones in the face of relevant heterogeneity. When one size does not fit all, it is best to adopt more than one size. No good travel website offers the same defaults for everyone. A health insurance plan that fits many people is unlikely to fit everybody, and hence personalization will produce far more accuracy. If a retirement plan that suits people under the age of forty is not sensible for people over the age of sixty, choice architects should try to personalize retirement plans.

Fourth, personalized default rules have some large advantages over active choosing, because they produce increases in accuracy without requiring people to devote the time and effort to choosing. It is tempting to say that personalized default rules are the best of both worlds, because they have the virtues of active choosing without having the downsides. That view is far too strong, in part because learning and agency can be important, but there is a lot of truth to this optimistic view. Personalized default rules deserve serious consideration whenever choice architects are both informed and trustworthy.

Fifth, mandates and bans have a legitimate place, certainly when harm to others is involved. But if the goal is to protect people against their own mistakes, there should be a presumption against mandates; the presumption can be overcome only with a clear demonstration that mandates will improve people's welfare. Of course it is true that default rules are not an adequate response to the problem of violent crime, and to handle the problem of pollution, it is necessary to go beyond defaults. But when there is no harm to others, we should begin with approaches that preserve freedom of choice. (I realize that this proposition leaves many unanswered questions, which I will take up in due course.)

One of my basic claims is that in the future, personalized default rules will be increasingly available, and for good reason. In ordinary life, family members and friends adopt, every day and in ways large and small (and often unconsciously), the functional equivalent of personalized default rules. They assume, reasonably enough, that people will want in the future what they have wanted in the past. Or perhaps they assume that people will want the same kinds of variety and surprise in the future that they have enjoyed in the past.

For example, spouses and close friends select default options for restaurants, vacation spots, romance, and even conversations, subject to opt-out. If people like routine, spouses and friends choose routine as the default. If people like surprises, they choose surprises. As information accumulates about people's actual choices, many private and public institutions will be in a position to provide personalized default rules. For better or for worse (and mostly for better), the age of personalized default rules is upon us.

THE PLAN

The book comes in three parts. Part I focuses on human behavior. Chapter 1 explores why default rules matter, emphasizing the roles of inertia, suggestion, and loss aversion. Chapter 2 discusses default rules that do not stick. It shows that when people are willing to choose, and have clear preferences that predate the default rule, they will go their own way. This chapter also shows that when self-interested firms dislike a default rule, they might be able to get people to depart from it.

Part II turns to moral and political questions. Chapter 3 investigates how to choose a default rule. It urges that the central goal should be to identify the approach that informed choosers would select. The basic idea is that if we know what such choosers would select, we know what approach would promote social welfare, properly understood. This chapter also investigates the problem of bad defaults, which are all around us.

Chapter 4 turns to active choosing and the circumstances in which it is desirable. Active choosing has an especially honored position in liberal political thought, and for good reasons. Chapter 5 investigates the other side of the coin: why and when people choose not to choose. It shows that when people make that choice, it is a form of paternalism to call for active choosing.

Part III turns to the future. Chapter 6 explores personalized default rules and explains why they are increasingly pervasive. Chapter 7 discusses predictive shopping, embodied in the idea that sellers may know what you want before you do. Chapter 7 introduces some survey evidence about people's reactions to predictive shopping—showing that most people reject it, but that a lot of people embrace it. Chapter 8 discusses the role of coercion and argues for a presumption in favor of freedom of choice. The conclusion offers a general summary of the argument.

PART I

HUMAN BEHAVIOR

[1]

DECIDING BY DEFAULT

When people choose not to choose, they often favor, and rely on, default rules. My goal here is to give a sense of the importance, the pervasiveness, and the potential of such rules. As we will see, default rules often turn out to be decisive. A central question is this: Why, exactly, are defaults so "sticky," in the sense that people tend not to alter them, even if it is easy for them to do so? To answer that question, it will be useful to provide a few additional illustrations. For the moment, I shall be dealing only with impersonal default rules. In part III, I will turn to more personalized alternatives.

DEFAULTS IN ACTION: A VERY BRIEF TOUR

Paper. Human beings use a lot of paper, and paper requires use of a large number of trees. Suppose that a private or public institution wants both to save money and to protect the environment by reducing its use of paper. It could educate its employees about the potential value of reducing paper use ("just the facts"). It could try moral suasion by appealing to economic and environmental values; maybe it could make people feel a bit guilty, or ashamed, for using a lot of paper. Following standard economic prescriptions, it could impose some kind of charge or fee for paper use. Or it could impose ceilings on the total amount of paper used by relevant individuals or groups (with an inventive if unwieldy approach being a kind of cap-and-trade system, with a total "cap" and permission for people to trade with one another).

But consider a much simpler intervention: Change the institution's default printer setting from "print on a single page" to "print on front and back." A few years ago, Rutgers University adopted such a default. In the first three years of the new default, paper consumption was reduced by well over 55 million sheets, which amounted to a 44 percent reduction, the equivalent of 4,650 trees.[1] A natural field experiment at a large Swedish university also found a substantial reduction, with the significant and immediate effect of a 15 percent drop in paper consumption.[2] That effect stayed stable over time. (The sustained effect is worth underlining; the changes introduced by default rules tend not to diminish over time.)

It is evident that if private and public institutions decided in favor of a simple change of the default, they would have a large impact on paper usage. Many people use far more paper than they need only because of the "single page" default; a change would produce significant savings at negligible costs in terms of convenience and reading habits. At least in the face of weak preferences, the default has a large effect even though the costs of switching are exceedingly small.

Notably, that large effect occurs despite the fact that strong efforts to encourage people to use double-sided printing have essentially no impact. (There is a potential lesson here about the limited consequences of both encouragement and education, at least in some contexts.) Even more notably, the Swedish study concludes

1. See *Print Management Information*, RUTGERS UNIV., http://www.nbcs.rutgers.edu/ccf/main/print/transition.php (last updated April 11, 2012).
2. See Johan Egebark & Mathias Ekström, *Can Indifference Make the World Greener?* 3 (Research Inst. of Ind. Econ., Working Paper No. 975, 2013), *available at* http://papers.ssrn.com/id=2324922.

that the effect of the double-sided default much exceeds the likely effect of a 10 percent tax on paper products, which would produce a modest 2 percent reduction in paper use. Here as elsewhere, the simple switch in the default is both more effective and less costly than the economic incentive.

Taxi tips. In a number of cities, taxicabs have installed a credit card touchscreen. The screen sometimes suggests three possible tips by making them visible and easily available for customers to select with a quick "touch." In New York City, the suggested amounts are usually 20 percent, 25 percent, or 30 percent for rides of more than $15. People are free to give a larger tip, a smaller tip, or no tip at all, but it is easiest just to touch one of the three conspicuous options.

The touchscreen makes everything simpler and faster, but it also creates a set of defaults. To be sure, the suggested tips are not precisely that, because they do not establish what happens if people do nothing. Any tip requires some kind of effort. But the touchscreen does, in a sense, establish default tips. To depart from them, customers have to do at least a little bit of extra thinking and some extra work, and for that reason it might be expected that the defaults will affect the tips that drivers receive. Do they?

The economists Kareem Haggag and Giovanni Paci compiled data on more than 13 million New York taxi rides.[3] To test the effect of the defaults, they examined data from two companies that were contracted to provide credit card machines to New York City taxis. One company provided somewhat lower defaults of 15 percent, 20 percent, and 25 percent. Do people give lower tips when presented with these lower defaults? The other company, with the higher defaults, provided lower default percentages for fares under $15. Do those lower percentages reduce tips?

---

3. Kareen Haggag & Giovanni Paci, *Default Tips*, 6 Am. Econ. J.: Applied Econ. 1 (2014).

The main finding was that the higher default tips led to significant increases—by an average of more than 10 percent. That's a pretty major effect. If a driver makes $6,000 in tips in a year, the higher defaults lead to a $600 raise—and the taxi industry as a whole will receive many millions of dollars of additional revenue annually. Notably, the relatively high defaults also had an unintended side effect: Customers were 1.7 percent more likely to tip zero. Apparently some people get mad and give nothing. The backlash effect is not huge, and drivers are still significantly ahead on balance. But it is reasonable to speculate that higher default tips would increase the probability of zero tips, and that speculation, along with the backlash finding, is suggestive about when people will reject the default. Nonetheless, the central finding is clear, and it is that default tips have a significant impact. In any city, taxi drivers can obtain a nice raise if their company installs touchscreens that take credit cards and suggest tips that are higher than the current norm.

Insurance. In the context of auto insurance, an unplanned, natural experiment showed that for financial matters, default rules can be very sticky.[4] Pennsylvania offered a default insurance plan containing an unqualified right to sue and a relatively high annual premium. Purchasers could choose to switch to a new plan and save some money simply by "selling" the unqualified right to sue and paying a lower annual premium. By contrast, New Jersey's default program included a relatively low premium and no right to sue. In New Jersey, purchasers were allowed to switch from that program and "buy" the right to sue by paying a higher premium.

---

4. *See,* Eric J. Johnson et al., *Framing, Probability Distortions, and Insurance Decisions* [hereinafter *Framing*], *in* CHOICES, VALUES, AND FRAMES 224, 238 (Daniel Kahneman & Amos Tversky eds., 2000); *see also* Colin F. Camerer, *Prospect Theory in the Wild* (asserting that default rules establish a "reference point" from which people are reluctant to move), *in* CHOICES, VALUES, AND FRAMES, *supra,* at 288, 294–95; Cass R. Sunstein, *Switching the Default Rule,* 77 N.Y.U. L. REV. 106, 113 (2002) (explaining the effect of default rules in employment law).

There is no reason to think that with respect to automobile insurance, the people of Pennsylvania have systemically different preferences from the people of New Jersey. Most people lack strong preferences on whether it is worthwhile to pay for the right to sue; that is a complicated question, and you have to do a fair bit of work to answer it. And indeed in both cases, the default rule tended to stick, leading to very different outcomes in the two states. A strong majority accepted both default rules, with only about 20 percent of New Jersey drivers acquiring the full right to sue and 75 percent of Pennsylvanians retaining it. Hence the different defaults produced large differences in the insurance packages in the two states. Experiments confirm this basic effect, showing that people value the right to sue far more when it is presented as part of the default package.[5]

In a major testimonial to the economic importance of defaults, the selection of the default in Pennsylvania produced $140 million annually in additional insurance payments—and an aggregate amount of well over $2 billion since 1991![6]

Privacy. All over the world, people are vigorously debating privacy rights on the Internet. If you are surfing the web, should the sites you visit or the social media you use be able to track you and to share with others what they know about you? What about your tastes in music and books? What about your emotions, as reflected in the things you click on or choose to share on Facebook or Twitter? People have strong views on these questions. Some people believe that there should be a strong presumption in favor of privacy, to be overcome only when people offer an explicit and unambiguous statement of consent. On this view, the default rule should be protective of privacy. If people have not affirmatively waived their right to privacy, they should have privacy.

5. Johnson et al., *supra* note 4, at 235–38.
6. Eric J. Johnson & Daniel G. Goldstein, *Decisions by Default, in* THE BEHAVIORAL FOUNDATIONS OF POLICY 417, 417–18 (Eldar Shafir ed., 2013).

Other people emphasize that on the Internet, information sharing is an affirmative good, because it ensures that people can learn from one another. If people are sharing information, they can find out about all sorts of things—goods, services, experiences, opportunities, political abuses, even freedom. If people are able to know that certain sites are very popular, or that their fellow citizens are showing an interest in certain goods or points of view, they can learn a great deal. On this view, so-called privacy safeguards can be a big mistake, and even undo much of what makes the Internet so extraordinary, because such safeguards create a kind of prisoner's dilemma in which individually rational choices, protecting privacy, produce collective harm—in the form of reduced information about consumer goods, social risks, and political affairs. Privacy is smart for each but dumb for all. The conclusion is that the default rule should support information sharing.

The debates are heated ones and reasonable people can be found on all sides. Whatever the outcome of these debates, there is every reason to think that privacy rights and information sharing will be greatly affected by the default rule. In fact, the default rule might make all the difference.

Suppose that a public or private institution says that information about your behavior (for example, the websites you visit) will not be shared with other people *unless you click on a button to allow information sharing*. Now suppose instead that the same institution says that such information will be shared *unless you click on a button to forbid such sharing*. Will the results be the same? Far from it.[7]

---

7. *See* Eric Johnson et al., *Defaults, Framing and Privacy: Why Opting In-Opting Out*, 13 Marketing Letters 5, 9 (2002) (finding that protection of privacy is much affected by the default rule); *see also* Rebecca Balebako et al., Nudging Users Towards Privacy on Mobile Devices (2011) (unpublished manuscript), *available at* http://www.andrew.cmu.edu/user/pgl/paper6.pdf (reviewing the literature on defaults in privacy decisionmaking). For some significant qualifications, see Lauren Willis, *Why Not Privacy by Default?*, 29 Berkeley Tech. L.J. 61 (2014).

If people are asked whether they want to sacrifice privacy and opt in to information sharing, a lot of them will decline—perhaps on the ground that if their privacy is now protected, they do not want to sacrifice that protection. Efforts to convince them to do so may not be effective, especially because people are averse to losses (a point to which I will return), and a loss of privacy is not exactly welcome. In addition, a lot of people will simply ignore the question—perhaps because they are busy, inattentive, confused, or distracted or because they do not want to focus on it. In either case, their information will not be shared.

If, by contrast, people are asked whether they want to opt out of information sharing and protect their privacy, a lot of them will also decline or will ignore the question, perhaps because they are busy and inattentive or perhaps because they do not want to lose the potential advantages of such sharing. This is especially likely if they have to think a little bit, read something complicated, and form a preference in order to decide whether to switch. In that case, their information will be shared.

The upshot is that in the domain of privacy on the Internet, much depends on the default rule. If a web browser defaults people into privacy-protective settings, the outcomes will be very different from what they will be if people have to select privacy settings every time. Consider, for example, the recent choice architecture on Google Chrome. People are allowed to select "Incognito," but it is not the default, and users cannot easily make it into the default; the technology does not facilitate that. Users must choose to select "go Incognito" every time they log on. As a result, people go Incognito a lot less.

Google is undoubtedly aware of this, and it adopts a choice architecture that enlists inertia on behalf of information-sharing. Google does so in part because it has an economic interest in using what is known as a "reverting" default—a default that can be changed but that reverts to the choice that architects prefer, thus requiring another change on each visit. I shall discuss the importance of reverting defaults in other contexts.

Vacation time. Might people's workplace benefits, such as vacation time and health care, depend on the legal default rule? By this point, you will not be surprised to hear that the answer is yes.

To see how, consider a simple experiment I conducted a few years ago.[8] The experiment involved about 150 law students, with 75 answering one of two questions. Note that the two questions were not unrealistic. Law students are very much in the position of trading off variables in the selection of work, and both vacation time and salary matter to their decisions.

Question 1:

Imagine that you have accepted a job with a law firm in a large city. Your salary will be $120,000. Under state law, all companies must provide nonmanagerial employees, including associates at law firms, with a minimum of two weeks in vacation time each year.

Suppose that the firm that you have chosen tells you that it will allow you to have two extra weeks of vacation, but at a somewhat reduced salary. What is the most that you would be willing to pay, in reduced salary, to obtain those two extra weeks of vacation time? (Assume that no adverse consequences could possibly come to you from bargaining for that extra vacation time.)

Question 2:

Imagine that you have accepted a job with a law firm in a large city. Your salary will be $120,000. Under state law, all companies must

8. Sunstein, *supra* note 4, at 113–14.

provide nonmanagerial employees, including associates at law firms, with a nonwaivable minimum of two weeks in vacation time each year. State law also provides that all companies must provide nonmanagerial employees, including associates at law firms, with a waivable extra two weeks in vacation time each year. The extra two weeks can be waived only as a result of "explicit, noncoerced agreements" between the parties.

Suppose that the firm that you have chosen would be willing to pay you a certain amount in extra salary to get you to waive your right to the two extra weeks in vacation time. What is the least that the firm would have to pay you, in extra salary, to give up those two extra weeks? (Assume that no adverse consequences could possibly come to you from your refusal to waive, or from your demanding a high amount to waive.)

The results were dramatic. If the legal default rule does not include more vacation time, people will not pay a great deal to "buy" it. If the legal default rule includes more vacation time, people will demand a great deal to give it up. More specifically, people's median willingness to pay (question 1) was $6,000, whereas people's median willingness to accept (question 2) was $13,000.

This two-to-one difference is found in many places.[9] If people are asked whether they want to sell a good that they already own, they often name a price that is about twice what they would be willing to pay if they did not have it. At least this is so for goods that do not have a self-evident monetary value. Here is the key point: Whether they own a good in the first place or have to buy it will often depend on the default rule.

---

9. *See* RICHARD THALER, QUASI-RATIONAL ECONOMICS (1995).

WHY?

A great deal of research explores exactly why default rules have such a large effect on outcomes.[10] In some cases, the option to opt out is not readily visible, and so people have to do some work to find it. In such cases, it is easiest just to stick with the default, because people do not even know that they can change it. In other cases, opting out has a real cost, because choice architects do not want people to switch and will impose significant burdens on those who try to do so. Alternatively, people might be ill-informed or confused, and their lack of information or confusion might lead them to stick with the status quo. If you do not have clarity about the underlying problem, you might let things stay where they are and move on the other matters. But even when these factors are absent, and even when it is easy to switch the default, it tends to stick, and for three principal reasons.

THE POWER OF INERTIA

The basic problem. The first involves inertia and procrastination (sometimes described as "effort" or an "effort tax").[11] To change the

---

10. *See, e.g.,* Gabriel D. Carroll et al., *Optimal Defaults and Active Decisions,* 124 Q.J. ECON. 1639, 1641–43 (2009) (studying the effect on outcomes when a firm switched to an auto-enrollment 401(k) plan); William G. Gale, J. Mark Iwry, & Spencer Walters, *Retirement Savings for Middle- and Lower-Income Households: The Pension Protection Act of 2006 and the Unfinished Agenda* (exploring the effects of default rules on 401(k) plans), *in* AUTOMATIC 11, 13–14 (William G. Gale et al. eds., 2009); Isaac M. Dinner et al., Partitioning Default Effects: Why People Choose Not to Choose 3 (Nov. 28, 2010) (unpublished manuscript), *available at* http://papers.ssrn.com/id=1352488 (examining "no-action" defaults).

11. *See* Johnson & Goldstein, *supra* note 6, at 420–21 (exploring "effort tax"); *see also* Jeffrey R. Brown et al., The Downside of Defaults 20–21 (Sept. 16, 2011) (unpublished

default rule, you have to make an active choice to reject that rule. You have to focus on and answer the relevant question—whether you should be enrolled in a savings plan, whether you should have green energy, whether you would gain or lose from a privacy policy, or whether you should give a particular tip. Especially (but not only) if people are busy, or if the question is difficult or technical, or even if it merely lacks a self-evident answer, it is tempting to defer the decision or not to make it at all. In view of the power of inertia and the tendency to procrastinate, you might simply continue with the status quo.

Steve Krug's superb book on website design has just the right title: *Don't Make Me Think*.[12] Krug poses this question: "What's the most important thing I should do if I want to make sure my site or app is easy to use?" His answer? His title. He urges that when a web page is well designed, "I should be able to 'get it'—what it is and how I use it—without expending any effort thinking about it." Krug acknowledges that people sometimes enjoy puzzles, especially when they want to be challenged or diverted, but "as a rule, people don't *like* to puzzle over how to do things." Default rules are effective in part for this reason.

Consider in this regard a study of television viewing, where inertia exerts a powerful force.[13] As programs become more popular, the programs that follow them also become more popular, simply because the current channel is the default. In Italy, a 10 percent increase in the popularity of a program leads to a remarkable 2–4 percent increase in the audience for the following program.

manuscript), *available at* http://www.nber.org/aging/rrc/papers/orrc11-01.pdf (citing procrastination as one reason for effects of defaults).

12. Steve Krug, Don't Make Me Think Revisited: A Common Sense Approach to Web and Mobile Usability (2014).

13. Constança Esteves-Sorenson & Fabrizio Perretti, *Micro-Costs: Inertia in Television Viewing*, 122 Econ. J. 867, 868 (2012).

A striking finding is that stations exploit this behavior when scheduling their programs—and if they did not, they would lose up to 40 percent of their profits.

For television programs, of course, viewers simply need to push a button to switch the channel, and channel-switching is the furthest thing from difficult. Opting in or opting out of default rules might be equally easy. But in many cases, it involves some thinking and some risk. The default rule might stick simply because people do not want to engage in that thinking and take that risk. And even if they want to do so, they might decide that they will do so tomorrow—and tomorrow never comes.

Within economics and the economic analysis of law, it is usual to refer to "transactions costs," which can impose significant barriers to action. For example, it takes time and effort to enter into a contract, and people may not want to expend either of these, especially if they have to assemble information in order to do so. Because of transactions costs, a lot of mutually beneficial contracts do not ever get made. When default rules stick, transactions costs may well be the reason. People might lack the knowledge or the time to change them. But behavioral economists have added a different point. Even when transactions costs are zero or close to it, inertia is quite powerful, and people will stick with the default—whatever it is—even if they do not know that they like it, and indeed even if they know that they do not like it. (As we will see, things are different if they hate it.)

The human brain. What about the human brain? Are there neurological markers of the effects of defaults? A study of the brain, using fMRI scanning, confirms the intuition that default settings are especially important in complex situations.[14] In this study, participants acted as line judges in a tennis match. An established default

---

14. Stephen M. Fleming et al., *Overcoming Status Quo Bias in the Human Brain*, 107 Proc. Nat'l Acad. Sci. 6005, 6005 (2010).

was provided to participants, suggesting that the ball was either in or out. But if the participants saw things differently, they could override the default. As the decision became harder—because the call was closer—people became more likely not to alter the default. By itself, that's not so surprising. The more striking finding was that the region of the brain associated with more difficult decisions (the inferior frontal cortex) was more active when people rejected the default. This finding has general implications. It confirms that default rules are more likely to stick when the underlying decision is hard and thus that such rules will be especially powerful in technical or unfamiliar areas. It also suggests that the power to opt out is less likely to be a useful safeguard in such circumstances. Consistent with this suggestion, complexity has sometimes been treated as an independent reason for the power of defaults, though it might be more properly treated as an amplifier of inertia, or an increase in the "effort tax."[15]

Two kinds of effort. It is important to make a distinction here between two kinds of effort. The first is the effort involved in focusing on the problem and the default rule and on whether to change it. Even if you begin with an initial preference of some kind, any such effort may be at least mildly unwelcome. Maybe you would prefer green energy to gray energy, but maybe you aren't excited about spending a lot of extra money, and it's just not worthwhile to investigate the whole question. Maybe you would like to give a bit more money to charity, but you don't want to take the trouble to do so. Life is short, people are busy, and there are other and more enjoyable or more pressing things to do.

15. See John Beshears et al., *The Importance of Default Options for Retirement Saving Outcomes: Evidence from the USA* (arguing that lower participation in opt-in savings plans is a result of the complexity of making an optimal savings plan decision), in LESSONS FROM PENSION REFORMS IN THE AMERICAS 59, 74–75 (Stephen Kay & Tapen Sinha eds., 2008).

The second and perhaps more interesting kind of effort is that involved in *forming a preference in the first place*. People may not yet have developed a preference about whether to enroll in some savings or exercise program or to start some new activity. The default rule may help to construct that preference; it informs and even creates their judgment about what they want. People might have to engage in some real work even to decide what their preferences are. Consider, for example, the question of which health insurance plan is best; people may not have a preference on that count, and it may take considerable work to produce one. Maybe people don't want to undertake that work.

The importance of both kinds of effort in making defaults more likely to stick is demonstrated by evidence that when people are tired, they are more likely to stay with the default.[16] Suppose that you have made a number of decisions in the last hour and then are asked to make yet another. When people are suffering from "decision fatigue," they are even more likely to stick with the default. An important implication is that if time is especially scarce or if people have many decisions to make, the default will be particularly appealing, because something like the "yeah, whatever" heuristic will be hard to resist.

This is a significant point for both governments and firms to keep in mind. Psychologists have studied the effects of "cognitive load," which refers to the sheer amount of cognitive work that people are doing at a particular time.[17] If, for example, you have recently tried to answer some difficult set of arithmetic problems or are asked to keep a series of numbers in your mind, your subsequent

16. See Jonathan Levav et al., *Order in Product Customization Decisions: Evidence from Field Experiments*, 118 J. Pol. Econ. 274, 277 (2010) ("'[C]hoice overload' can prompt people to forgo making a choice altogether").

17. Fred Paas, Alexander Renkl, & John Sweller, *Cognitive Load Theory and Instructional Design: Recent Developments*, 38 Educational Psychologist 1–4 (2003).

choices and behavior may well be affected. With a high cognitive load, you might be more likely to select chocolate cake instead of carrots, and you might generally opt for the path of least resistance. In the face of a high cognitive load, a default rule might prove especially sticky—which suggests that people who are especially busy, or who are otherwise burdened, will be particularly prone to accept default rules.

Not too cold. With respect to the effects of inertia, consider the finding that a change in the default thermostat setting had a major effect on employees at the Organization for Economic Co-operation and Development.[18] During winter, a 1°C decrease in the default caused a significant reduction in the average chosen setting. The best explanation is that in light of the power of inertia, most employees did not find it worthwhile to bother to alter the default. This interpretation is supported by an especially noteworthy finding: When choice architects reduced the default setting by 2°C, the reduction in the average chosen setting was actually *smaller*, apparently because sufficient numbers of employees thought that it was too cold and returned the setting to the one that they preferred. In the face of clear discomfort, inertia is overcome.

I think this study is profound, and I will return to it. It is profound because it suggests that a default rule will stick even if it is not entirely comfortable—but if people start to feel really cold, they will reject it. There are large lessons here about the role of default rules and the power of inertia in many settings.

The same study suggests another point as well. In the workplace, people might well face social influences, especially if they think that their behavior is being observed. If you are given an environmentally friendly default rule, you might not change it, at least not if your

---

18. See Zachary Brown et al., *Testing the Effects of Defaults on the Thermostat Settings of OECD Employees*, 39 ENERGY ECON. 128 (2013).

colleagues will see that you are doing so. Individual shame, guilt, and personal conscience can, of course, operate in the absence of a default rule. But sometimes shame, guilt, and conscience are not enough to change behavior, and observation by others can make all the difference—at least if people are not terribly cold.

DEFAULT RULES AS INFORMATIONAL SIGNALS

The second factor involves what people might see as the *informational signal* that the default rule provides. If choice architects have explicitly chosen that rule, many people will believe that they have been given an implicit recommendation, and by people who know what they are doing. If so, they will think that they should not depart from it and go their own way, unless they have private information that is reliable and that would justify a change.[19] Going your own way is risky, and you might not want to do it unless you are really confident that you should.

A signal. Suppose that the default choice is green energy or that a public or private employer automatically enrolls employees into a particular pension or health care plan. Such defaults tempt many people to think that experts, or sensible authorities, believe that these are the right courses of action. In deciding whether to opt out,

---

19. *See* Brigitte C. Madrian & Dennis F. Shea, *The Power of Suggestion: Inertia in 401(k) Participation and Savings Behavior,* 116 Q.J. ECON. 1149, 1182 (2001) (suggesting that employees are more likely to invest in a 401(k) retirement plan if the default rule is to allocate part of their income because "employees view the default investment allocation under automatic enrollment as implicit advice from the company on 'the best' allocation of one's retirement assets"); Craig R. M. McKenzie, Michael J. Liersch, & Stacey R. Finkelstein, *Recommendations Implicit in Policy Defaults,* 17 PSYCHOL. SCI. 414, 418–19 (2006) (describing experiments in which policymakers' preferences were reflected in the default option provided to decisionmakers, who were in turn unlikely to deviate from the default). Of course, it is not true that all defaults are chosen because they produce the best outcomes for choosers.

you might trust the choice architects well enough to follow their lead. Many people appear to think that the default has been chosen by someone who is wise, decent, or smart and for a good reason. Especially if you lack experience or expertise, you might simply defer to a choice that has been made for you.

Indeed, there is strong evidence that lack of information on the part of choosers, including lack of information about alternatives, helps to account for the power of defaults.[20] This evidence suggests that default rules are less likely to have an effect when people consider themselves to be experienced or expert in the matter at hand.

In fact, findings to precisely this effect have been made in a study of environmental economists, who reject selected defaults in the environmental area.[21] The experiment involved CO_2 offsets. The subjects were participants at the annual meeting of the European Association of Environmental and Resource Economists in June 2008. Participants were not allowed to complete their registration for the meeting unless they indicated their preferences with respect to offsets. As the experiment was constructed, people were randomly assigned to one of three conditions. In the first, compensation was the default option, in the form of a full offset. People could opt out by saying, "I do not want to compensate for my CO_2 emissions." In the second condition, people were given noncompensation as the default and they had to opt in. The third treatment involved "active choosing," in which participants had to make an active choice whether or not to offset their travel.

Remarkably, there were no statistically significant differences among the three treatments. Environmental experts know

---

20. See Brown et al., supra note 11, at 3 ("[A] lack of adequate information about decision alternatives is a significant driver of the likelihood of default").
21. Åsa Löfgren et al., Are Experienced People Affected by a Pre-Set Default Option—Results from a Field Experiment, 63 J. ENVTL. ECON. & MGMT. 66 (2012).

what they prefer. In general, they favor offsets. They do what they want, regardless of whether they are facing opt-out or opt-in or are engaged in active choosing.

Trust and information. The implication, of course, is that when people do not know what they want, the default is more likely to stick. In another study, over half of those who stuck with the default specifically mentioned their own lack of information as one of their reasons for doing so.[22] It follows that if choosers do not trust the choice architect, they will be far more likely to opt out. Indeed, there is evidence for this proposition as well.[23] Here, then, is a possible method for testing whether inertia or instead perceived endorsement is making the default rule stick. If people opt out when they do not trust the choice architect, then inertia is not so powerful.

An asymmetry. At the same time, there is an important qualification to the "informational signal" explanation for the power of default rules, which involves a major difference in how people react to enrollment and nonenrollment.[24] More specifically, people believe that *automatic enrollment conveys information about what is sensible or best—but that automatic nonenrollment does not.* If people are automatically enrolled in a health care or a savings plan, they assume that someone has decided that it is in their interest to be enrolled. But when they are *not* automatically enrolled, they make no such assumption. Nonenrollment conveys no signal at all.

22. *See* Brown et al., *supra* note 11, at 19 ("In total, 51.3 percent of the defaulters chose at least one information-related problem as an explanation for their default behavior").

23. *See* David Tannenbaum & Peter H. Ditto, Information Asymmetries in Default Options 11–17 (unpublished manuscript), *available at* https://webfiles.uci.edu/dtannenb/www/documents/default%20information%20asymmetries.pdf (describing a study in university classrooms that found a positive correlation between students' trust in their instructor and their decision to stick with a default scheme of assignment due dates).

24. *Id.* at 17.

The reason is that people take automatic enrollment as a deliberate decision by the choice architects. They believe that the architects would adopt automatic enrollment only if there was a good reason for it. By contrast, people take nonenrollment as reflecting simple inaction, without any supporting judgment, and hence as not conveying any information. This is of course a perfectly plausible inference. When the system is set up so that you have to take steps to enroll, there is no justification for concluding that an employer, or anyone else, thinks that you should not enroll.

This finding suggests that many people are willing to make some kind of judgment about the reason for the default rule. They understand automatic enrollment to be motivated by a belief that enrollment is a good idea. But they think that nonenrollment reflects no particular motivation and does not signal a belief about what is best. (Note that viewing nonenrollment as a result of mere inaction is also a plausible inference.) This point bears in turn on the question of paternalism. Nonenrollment is certainly a default; it represents an initial allocation and it tends to be sticky. But because people do not understand it to suggest any view on the part of choice architects, it is neutral along an important dimension, whereas automatic enrollment is not. Some people who reject paternalism, even of the softer or more libertarian kinds, might prefer nonenrollment for that reason.

The important empirical finding is that while automatic enrollment is sticky as a result of both inertia and endorsement, automatic nonenrollment is sticky only as a result of the former. An implication, with experimental support, is that automatic enrollment will be particularly sticky when people trust the choice architects, but not so much when that trust is low.[25] That finding makes perfect sense. When people think that choice architects have set up an automatic enrollment for illegitimate reasons, they will be entirely

25. *Id.* at 17.

willing to reject that course. But when trust is low, similar swings should not be seen for nonenrollment simply because it is not taken to reflect a judgment on the part of the choice architect. And in fact, the research does not find any such swings.[26]

LOSS AVERSION AND REFERENCE POINTS

To understand the third explanation of why default rules are so powerful, consider the behavioral finding of *loss aversion*—one of the most important and robust in all of behavioral science. The basic conclusion is that people dislike losses far more than they like corresponding gains.[27] In general, human beings will do a lot to avoid losses from the status quo. The default rule establishes the status quo; it determines the reference point for counting changes as losses or as gains.

For a clean demonstration of the powerful impact of loss aversion, consider a study of the District of Columbia's small 5-cent tax on disposable grocery bags.[28] The study showed that despite its

---

26. *Id.* at 4.
27. *See* Daniel Kahneman, Jack L. Knetsch, & Richard H. Thaler, *Experimental Tests of the Endowment Effect and the Coase Theorem* (highlighting the phenomenon of loss aversion, where "losses are weighted substantially more than objectively commensurate gains"), *in* QUASI RATIONAL ECONOMICS 167, 169 (Richard H. Thaler ed., 1994); A. Peter McGraw et al., *Comparing Gains and Losses*, 21 PSYCHOL. SCI. 1438, 1443–44 (2010) (concluding that loss aversion manifests itself even in tasks where gains and losses are placed in the same context). Vivid evidence of loss aversion can be found in David Card & Gordon B. Dahl, *Family Violence and Football: The Effect of Unexpected Emotional Cues on Violent Behavior*, 126 Q.J. ECON. 103, 105–06, 130–35 (2011) (finding an increase in domestic violence after a favored football team suffers an upset loss).
28. Tatiana A. Homonoff, Can Small Incentives Have Large Effects? The Impact of Taxes Versus Bonuses on Disposable Bag Use 2–4 (Mar. 27, 2013) (unpublished manuscript), *available at* http://www.princeton.edu/~homonoff/THomonoff_JobMarketPaper.pdf.

modesty, the tax has had a large effect in reducing disposable grocery bag use. People don't want to lose money, even if the amount that they would lose is small. Would a gain in the form of a small subsidy have a similar effect? Actually not. Before the implementation of the tax, stores offered customers a 5-cent bonus for using reusable bags; it had essentially no impact. The potential loss was what mattered, not the potential gain.

There is a general implication here. If the goal is to encourage behavior, should people be offered a bonus or instead be threatened with a penalty? It isn't very nice to threaten people, but a prospect of a loss tends to concentrate the mind, even if the loss is small.

For present purposes, the key point is that whether a loss or a gain is involved does not come from nature or from the sky. The default rule determines what counts as a loss and what counts as a gain. Here's a small example. Professional golfers are paid if they do well in tournaments. A stroke is a stroke; if you shoot 72, your score is the same whether you had eighteen consecutive pars or nine birdies and nine bogeys. (For nongolfers: a "par" is the score a good golfer is expected to get, whereas a "birdie" is one stroke better, and a "bogey" is one stroke worse.) Nonetheless, professional golfers do better when they are trying to make par than when they are shooting for birdie.[29] The reason is that par is, in a sense, the default, and you really don't want to lose a stroke to it. A birdie is good, maybe even great, but it's not as wonderful as a bogey is terrible. At least that is the apparent psychology of professional golfers—even if on the scoreboard a stroke is a stroke. One of the noteworthy features of this example is that what counts as par does not come from

29. Devin G. Pope & Maurice E. Schweitzer, *Is Tiger Woods Loss Averse? Persistent Bias in the Face of Experience, Competition, and High Stakes*, 101 AM. ECON. REV. 129, 129–57 (2011).

nature but is a matter of convention; the choice to select "3" as par rather than "4" establishes losses and gains.

To appreciate the power of loss aversion and its relationship to default rules, consider an ingenious study of teacher incentives.[30] Many people have been interested in encouraging teachers to do better to improve their students' achievements. The results of providing economic incentives are pretty mixed. Unfortunately, many of these efforts have failed.[31] But the relevant study enlists loss aversion by resetting the default. The authors gave teachers money in advance and told them that if their students did not show real improvements, *the teachers would have to give the money back.* The result was a significant increase in students' math scores—indeed, an increase equivalent to that produced by a major improvement in teacher quality. The underlying idea here is that with respect to salary, losses from the status quo are especially unwelcome, and people will work hard to avoid those losses.

The study confirms that what counts as a loss depends on the reference point, which is established by the default rule. Suppose that employees are receiving $5,000 per month in take-home salary, and the question is whether they want some of that amount to be deducted for savings. If so, many employees might decline. Who wants to lose a significant part of his take-home pay? But if the employer is giving the employees $4,800 per month in take-home salary and putting $200 per month into savings for them, many might not complain—and they might strongly resist the idea of taking away that $200 per month from savings. Who wants to lose her savings? With respect to the power of default rules, many

30. Roland G. Fryer, Jr., et al., *Enhancing the Efficacy of Teacher Incentives Through Loss Aversion: A Field Experiment* 2–3 (Nat'l Bureau of Econ. Research, Working Paper No. 18237, 2012), *available at* http://www.nber.org/papers/w18237.

31. Field experiments in the United States that have linked teacher pay to teacher performance "have shown small, if not negative, treatment effects." *Id.* at 2.

of the findings described thus far might well be a product of loss aversion.

In sum, loss aversion matters, and it helps to explain the effect of the default rule. Energy use and environmental protection are important illustrations. If the default rule favors energy-efficient light bulbs, and people are asked whether they want less efficient bulbs, then the loss (in terms of reduced efficiency) may loom large—and they will continue to purchase energy-efficient light bulbs.[32] But if the default rule favors less efficient (and initially less expensive) light bulbs, and people are asked whether they want to pay more for efficient ones, then the loss (in terms of upfront costs) may loom large—and people will show a tendency to favor less efficient light bulbs. For issues that involve the environment, default rules matter in part because of loss aversion.

It is important to emphasize that loss aversion is apparently hardwired into the human species (and other species as well); it can be found across a wide variety of people and situations. But context does matter. When men and women are made to feel especially self-protective because of a possible threat, they become even more loss averse. And here is one of the very few interventions that eliminates loss aversion: When men are asked to imagine a romantic situation and are thus aroused, they no longer display loss aversion. (Women do not show this effect.)[33]

32. Isaac M. Dinner et al., Partitioning Default Effects: Why People Choose Not to Choose 12-14 (Nov. 28, 2010) (unpublished manuscript), available at http://papers.ssrn.com/id=1352488 (examining "no-action" defaults).

33. See Yexin Jessica Li et al., Economic Decision Biases and Fundamental Motivations: How Mating and Self-Protection Alter Loss Aversion, 102 J. PERSONALITY AND SOC. PSYCHOL. 550 (2012). When people are able to regulate their emotions, they also show reduced loss aversion. See Peter Sokol-Hessner et al., Emotion Regulation Reduces Loss Aversion and Decreases Amygdala Responses to Losses, 8 SOC. COGNITIVE AND AFFECTIVE NEUROSCIENCE 341 (2013).

RESPONSIBILITY, GUILT, AND SHAME

The three factors just outlined are the major ones, but there are others.[34] In particular, a default rule might stick because people do not want to take responsibility. They choose not to choose for that reason. Suppose, for example, that people are defaulted into green energy. They might not change the default because they believe that doing so would be morally questionable, a violation of norms of good citizenship.[35] Perhaps they would refuse to opt in to green energy because they want to save money, or perhaps they would not select green energy under circumstances of active choosing. But if the default rule is good for the environment, they might stick with it in order to avoid shame or guilt. It is one thing not to opt in to an approach that is environmentally friendly. It is quite another to opt out in favor of an approach that is environmentally unfriendly.

This point holds in any case in which a decision has some kind of moral dimension, because active choices trigger feelings of responsibility far more than passive ones.[36] The most obvious examples

34. See Brown et al., *supra* note 11, at 18–21 (listing various reasons that may account for influence of defaults).

35. On the role of guilt, see Aristeidis Theotokis & Emmanoela Manganari, *The Impact of Choice Architecture on Sustainable Consumer Behavior: The Role of Guilt*, J. BUS. ETHICS (July 19, 2014), *available at* http://link.springer.com/article/10.100 7%2Fs10551-014-2287-4 (finding that opt-out default policies are more effective than opt-in policies in the environmental area, because they increase anticipated guilt).

36. *Id.* For a demonstration, see Bjorn Bartling & Urs Fischbacher, *Shifting the Blame: On Delegation and Responsibility*, 79 REV. ECON. STUD. 67 (2012). On people's preference for flipping a coin, as a way of avoiding responsibility, see Nadja Dwengler et al., Flipping A Coin: Theory and Evidence (2013) (unpublished manuscript), available at http://papers.ssrn.com/sol3/papers.cfm?abstract_id=2353282. Consider this suggestion, *id.* at 1: The "cognitive or emotional cost of deciding may outweigh the benefits that arise from making the optimal choice. For example, the decision-maker may prefer not to make a choice without having sufficient time and energy to think it through. Or, she

involve choices that affect other people. Return to default tips in taxis. If you reject a high default in favor of some lower amount, and if you do so actively, you might have a sense that you are violating a social norm and being a bit selfish and unkind. For that reason, you might not select that lower amount—even though you might have done so passively. Social norms also establish what counts as fair and what counts as cheating, and it is reasonable to think that people who would never actively choose to cheat might be willing to do so passively. A tennis player, John, might have a firm rule against cheating with respect to the score of a game or a set, but if his partner Thomas makes a mistake in John's favor, perhaps John will not correct him. And even if John would never cheat on his taxes, he might not correct the Internal Revenue Service if it sends him a check that he does not deserve. The basic point is that when people are choosing passively—as by default—the sense of personal responsibility is attenuated.

People also have a sense of responsibility to themselves. If the default portion size is small at meals, or if a restaurant or a cafeteria selects healthy default choices, you might not want to take responsibility for outcomes that could well compromise your health. You will not ask for a larger plate or for less healthy meals. But if you received one of these by default, you might not complain or ask to switch. A great deal of further work needs to be done on the relationship between feelings of responsibility and active or passive decisions—but the basic point is clear.

---

may not feel entitled to make it. Or, she may anticipate a possible disappointment about her choice that can arise after a subsequent resolution of uncertainty. Waiving some or all of the decision right may seem desirable in such circumstances even though it typically increases the chance of a suboptimal outcome."

DIVERSE EXPLANATIONS, DIVERSE CONCERNS

For choice architects, including policymakers in both private and public sectors, the explanation for the stickiness of the default rule may be relevant to the decision about whether to change it. Each explanation raises independent concerns.

Suppose that people do not alter the default rule because they believe that choice architects have implicitly endorsed it. In a way, that seems like a liberating idea for the architects, who might consider themselves free to adopt the default rule that they do in fact endorse. But there is a countervailing consideration. A great deal of research suggests that when trusted authorities tell people to do something, they become far more likely to do it, even if it is wrong and even if it involves cruelty. In Stanley Milgram's famous research, people were willing to follow an experiment's instruction to administer electric shocks to those who answered certain questions inaccurately.[37] (In fact the shocks were not real, but the subjects in the experiment did not know that.) Milgram emphasized the importance of "obedience to authority," and he believed that such obedience could lead people to do horrible things. The most persuasive explanations of Milgram's findings point to the fact that people believe that some experts are trustworthy, sensible, and reliable. It follows that when certain authorities seem to have expertise, people will follow them.[38]

---

37. *See* STANLEY MILGRAM, OBEDIENCE TO AUTHORITY: AN EXPERIMENTAL VIEW 1–12 (1974) (describing an experiment in which participants obeyed instructions to administer electric shocks to actors who were pretending to be volunteers in another room despite orders to increase the number of volts administered).

38. *See* CASS R. SUNSTEIN, WHY SOCIETIES NEED DISSENT 32–37 (2003) (summarizing the Milgram experiment and exploring it as a prominent example of individuals blindly following expertise).

Here, then, is a serious problem: Deferring to real or apparent expertise, people may follow authorities who set default rules, even if those rules are harmful, self-interested, or nefarious. To be sure, choice architects are unlikely to believe themselves to be nefarious, and so they will not be much moved by this concern. But from the social point of view, the power of authority and expertise might well argue in favor of institutional safeguards and perhaps call for active choosing in circumstances in which the choice architects cannot be trusted. Obedience has its downsides. I will return to this point.

If the default rule sticks as a result of inertia or loss aversion, the underlying concern is different. In such cases, there might seem to be a serious risk of manipulation, compromising human agency and even dignity. Perhaps choice architects are exploiting behavioral findings to produce their preferred outcomes.[39] Manipulation is a strong charge, and if choice architects are hiding what they are doing, it might be a compelling objection. For that reason, the default rule should be made public and ought not to be hidden in any way; if it is public, the charge of manipulation is less likely to be justified. Unless active choosing is required, some default rule has to be in place, and it does not make a lot of sense to take the inevitable default rule as a form of unacceptable manipulation. Is it really manipulative to have a system of automatic enrollment in a savings plan? More manipulative than to have automatic nonenrollment? Is it more manipulative to have a double-sided than a single-sided default for printing? So long as people are informed of what the

---

39. *See, e.g.,* Edward L. Glaeser, *Paternalism and Psychology,* 73 U. CHI. L. REV. 133, 136–39 (2006) (offering examples of how individuals' beliefs and opinions can be manipulated); Joshua D. Wright & Douglas H. Ginsburg, *Behavioral Law and Economics: Its Origins, Fatal Flaws, and Implications for Liberty,* 106 NW. U. L. REV. 1033, 1049 & n. 71 (2012) (citing literature studying how companies exploit cognitive biases).

default rule is, skeptics should hesitate before leveling a charge of manipulation.

But there is no question that choice architects often select default rules to produce outcomes that they think best, and it is also true that sometimes people pay no attention to default rules (and therefore stick with them). That can be a blessing, but it can also be a problem. At least in cases involving inadequately informed or untrustworthy choice architects, there is a strong argument on behalf of active choosing, not least from the standpoint of human dignity. I will return to that argument. First, however, it is important to understand why some default rules are pretty slippery—and why people choose anyway.

[2]

CHOOSING ANYWAY

In some circumstances, default rules do not stick. Consider an especially slippery default: marital names.[1]

When people marry, all states in the United States have the same default rule: Both men and women retain their premarriage surnames. But there is nothing inevitable about that default rule. It is easy to imagine alternatives. For example:

- The husband's surname stays the same and the wife's surname changes to that of her husband. Indeed, that approach, however discriminatory (and almost certainly unconstitutional), would mimic people's actual choices, at least in the United States.
- The husband's surname changes to that of his wife, and the wife's name stays the same.
- The spouses' surnames are hyphenated.
- The spouses' surnames are changed to Skywalker, or Obama, or Gaga, or Potatohead.

What are the effects of the current rule? In the overwhelming majority of cases, American men do stick with the default. Relatively

---

1. For a full discussion of defaults in the context of marital names, see generally Elizabeth F. Emens, *Changing Name Changing: Framing Rules and the Future of Marital Names*, 74 U. Chi. L. Rev. 761 (2007).

few men change their names. By contrast, the overwhelming majority of American women do so—for college graduates, 80 percent.[2] In that respect, the default rule seems to have relatively little impact on women. To be sure, the percentage of women who change their names might be even higher if they were defaulted into doing so. Nonetheless, it is revealing that most married women reject the default.

CLEAR PREFERENCES AND EXTREME DEFAULTS

Why doesn't the default rule stick for women? Four factors seem to be important. First, many women affirmatively want to change their names, and their desire is not unclear. This is not a complex or unfamiliar area in which people have vague or ambiguous preferences or have to work to ascertain their preferences. True, many women are undoubtedly affected by social norms, which some of them may wish to be otherwise; but all things considered, their preference is not unclear. When a social norm is strong, it may overwhelm the effect of the legal default rule—a point with general implications.

Second, the issue is highly salient to married women. It is not exactly in the background. Because marriage is a defined and defining event, the timing of the required action is relatively clear. Procrastination and inertia are therefore less important; the effort tax is well worth incurring.

Third, the change of name is, for some or many of those who do it, a kind of celebration. It is not the sort of activity that most women seek to defer, or see as an obligation or as a way of helping

2. *Id.* at 786.

their future selves. If people affirmatively like to choose—if choosing is fun or meaningful—a supposed "effort tax" is nothing of the sort. It may even be a kind of "effort subsidy." There is a larger lesson here about what happens when choosing is a benefit rather than a burden.

Fourth, keeping one's name can be a bit of a headache, especially (but not only) if one has children. If a wife has a different name from her husband, or vice versa, it might be necessary to offer explanations, to fill out paperwork, and to dispel confusion. With some private and public institutions, offering those explanations might be burdensome and time-consuming. For some women, life is made more difficult if they do not have the same name as their husbands. Social practices create a strong incentive to overcome the default. When the relevant conditions are met—clear preferences, clear timing, positive feelings about opt-in, and greater ease and simplicity from opt-in—the default rule is unlikely to matter much.[3]

Indeed, clear preferences are likely to be sufficient to ensure that the default rule will not stick. We have seen that preferences may be constructed by default rules, rather than antedating them. That is one reason that they matter. But if preferences are clear, the default rule has a much weaker effect. In such cases, inertia will be overcome. People will not be much moved by any suggestion that might be reflected in the default rule (and in the context of marital names, the default offers no such suggestion). Loss aversion will be far less relevant, in part because the clear preference, rather than the default rule, defines the reference point from which losses are measured.

Recall that when the default thermometer setting is 2°C colder in winter, people change it; when they're cold they know it, and they

---

3. Elizabeth Emens has offered a number of suggestions in the context of marital names. *Id.* at 829–36.

don't want to be cold. Or suppose that employees are automatically enrolled into a plan that puts 80 percent of their income into savings, or 60 percent of their income into their nation's treasury (after taxes), or 20 percent of their income into their worst enemy's savings account, or 10 percent of their income into the toilet.[4] Most employees in such plans will undoubtedly opt out. They will choose anyway.

A study in the United Kingdom found that most people opted out of a savings plan, admittedly less horrible than those just described, but with an unusually high default contribution rate (12 percent of pretax income).[5] Only about 25 percent of employees remained at that rate after a year, whereas about 60 percent of employees shifted to a lower default contribution rate. Notably, people with lower incomes were more likely to stay at the unusually high contribution rate, even though they might well have had stronger reasons to opt out, given that they had a greater need for resources in the present. Similar findings have been made elsewhere, with growing evidence that those who are less educated or less sophisticated are more likely to stick with the default—a point, and a problem, to which I will return.[6]

There are other situations in which the default rule does not have a large impact. Workers are not so much affected if a significant fraction of their tax refund is defaulted into U.S. savings bonds. In large numbers, they opt out, apparently because they have definite plans to spend their refunds and do not have much interest in

---

4. On using precommitment devices (such as putting a specified amount into a worst enemy's savings account), see generally IAN AYRES, CARROTS AND STICKS (2010).
5. John Beshears et al., The Limitations of Defaults (Sept. 15, 2010) (unpublished manuscript), *available at* http://www.nber.org/programs/ag/rrc/NB10-02,%20 Beshears,%20Choi,%20Laibson,%20Madrian.pdf.
6. Jeffrey R. Brown et al., The Downside of Defaults (Dec. 13, 2012) (unpublished manuscript), *available at* http://www.nber.org/aging/rrc/papers/orrc12-05.pdf.

putting their tax refunds into savings.[7] The central finding—that default rules will have a weaker effect, and potentially no effect, when people have a strong antecedent preference for a certain outcome—is both a warning and an opportunity. It is a warning because it suggests that the default rule may not have the hoped-for effect. It is an opportunity because it suggests that the ability to opt out can be an important safeguard against defaults that are unhelpful or affirmatively harmful.

For choosers who are deciding whether to reject a default rule, there are two important considerations. One involves their level of knowledge of alternatives; the other involves their level of trust in the choice architect. If choosers have information about approaches that differ from that in the default, they are of course more likely to consider whether to select one of them. And if choosers think that the choice architects are not trustworthy, they are also more likely to want to choose and far less likely to be influenced by them (though inertia may still have a powerful effect). Indeed, there is good evidence that people will switch if they distrust choice architects. In particular, a number of people reject automatic enrollment for that reason.[8] And we have seen that if people do not have preexisting preferences—if their preferences are effectively constructed by the choice architect—then they are highly likely to stay with the default.

---

7. *See* Erin T. Bronchetti et al., *When a Default Isn't Enough: Defaults and Saving Among Low-Income Tax Filers* 28–29 (Nat'l Bureau of Econ. Research, Working Paper No. 16887, 2011), *available at* http://www.nber.org/papers/w16887 (explaining that default manipulation did not have an impact on tax refund allocation to a savings bond where an individual previously intended to spend the refund). Note, however, that the "default" in this study consisted of a mere statement on a form with the option to opt out. *Id.* at 17–18. In such a case, the line between the use of such a "default" and active choosing is relatively thin.

8. *See* David Tannenbaum & Peter H. Ditto, Information Asymmetries in Default Options 11–17 (2014) (unpublished manuscript), *available at* http://home.uchicago .edu/~davetannenbaum/documents/default%20information%20asymmetries.pdf.

A PUZZLE

The simplest implication is that "extreme" defaults are less likely to stick. The more puzzling implication, based on the lower incomes of those who stayed with the default in the study just described, is that default rules may be more sticky for low-income workers than for higher-earning ones. Why?

One reason may be that low-income workers have a lot to worry about and so are less likely to take the trouble to think through and to alter the default rule.[9] For people without a lot of money, cognitive resources tend to be especially scarce, because they have to devote those resources to figuring out how to get by. Consider here the important finding that the state of being poor, and focusing on how to make ends meet, has a significant adverse effect on performance on an IQ test—roughly equivalent to that of having no sleep the night before taking the test.[10]

In these circumstances, an effort tax may have an especially large harmful effect on people who are already facing a large number of decisions and costs. Some fascinating work explores the general problem of "bandwidth" faced by people who are poor (or busy, hungry, or lonely).[11] Because of limited bandwidth, poor

9. *See* ABHIJIT BANERJEE & ESTHER DUFLO, POOR ECONOMICS 64–68 (2011) (explaining that people, especially the poor, postpone small costs necessary for long-term rewards in exchange for small rewards in the present); *see also* Anuj K. Shah et al., *Some Consequences of Having Too Little*, 338 SCIENCE 682–83 (2012) (describing some effects of attention neglect on low-income individuals); *cf.* Jacob Goldin & Tatiana Homonoff, *Smoke Gets in Your Eyes: Cigarette Tax Salience and Regressivity*, 5 AM. ECON. J.: ECON. POL'Y, 302, 331 (2013) (finding that low-income people pay more particular attention to taxes at the register than wealthier people). For a discussion of the effects of scarcity in depleting psychological resources of poor people, see generally SENDHIL MULLAINATHAN & ELDAR SHAFIR, SCARCITY: WHY HAVING TOO LITTLE MEANS SO MUCH (2013).

10. *See* MULLAINATHAN & SHAFIR, *supra* note 9.

11. *See id.*

people may attend only to what immediately requires their attention, and when faced with a default rule that is not self-evidently harmful, they may ignore it or say "yeah, whenever." For this reason, defaults should be especially sticky for those who are poor (or busy).

Low-income workers may also have less confidence in their own judgments and may allow the default allocation to stick for that reason. We have seen that when people are experienced, and hence know what they want, they are far less likely to be affected by the default rule. One reason is that for such people, the effort tax is worth incurring. Lacking confidence, poor people may not want to incur that tax.[12]

The fact that low-income workers have been found to be especially unlikely to opt out has important implications for the uses and limits of default rules. Among other things, it suggests a potential danger in both impersonal and personalized defaults, which may prove harmful but nonetheless stick. Suppose that distributional considerations matter—that policymakers care who is helped and who is hurt by default rules. For example, a default rule might be desirable on environmental grounds; it might favor green energy. But if the result of such a default rule is to impose particular burdens on poor people, who will not bother to opt out, then policymakers might not be so comfortable with that rule. Distributional considerations, and in particular harmful effects on poor people, may raise particular problems for certain default rules, at least if they are not in the interest of a number of people to whom they apply—a point to which I will return.

---

12. Note, however, that poor people are uniquely attentive to sales taxes levied at the register. Goldin & Homonoff, *supra* note 9, at 331. This finding suggests the possibility that in some domains, poor people may be especially attentive and hence more likely to opt out.

PROMPTING OPT-OUT

In some situations, defaults may not stick even though they *are* important safeguards. Imagine that self-interested people have a strong incentive to get their customers to opt in or out. If so, they might be able to take clever (fiendish?) steps to achieve their goals. They might be able to convince you to choose not for your benefit but for theirs.

Suppose that green energy is far less profitable than more conventional energy sources. If so, firms that sell conventional energy might well take aggressive steps to encourage people to opt out of any default rule in favor of green energy. Especially if those steps are not only aggressive but also behaviorally informed, they might well succeed; they might, for example, enlist loss aversion to encourage opt-out. A double-sided default setting on your printer might seem like a good idea, but for paper companies it is not exactly welcome, and they might be able to think of ways to encourage people to switch to a single-sided default. Here, then, is an important safeguard against ill-chosen defaults—but also a serious obstacle to public-interested efforts to use defaults to produce desirable outcomes.

The problem is not hypothetical. Consider the regulatory effort in 2010 by the Federal Reserve Board to protect consumers from high bank overdraft fees.[13] To provide that protection, the Board did not impose any mandate but instead regulated the default rule. It said that banks could not automatically enroll people in overdraft "protection" programs; instead, customers had to sign up. More particularly, the Board's regulation forbids banks from charging a fee for overdrafts from checking accounts unless the account holder

---

13. Requirements for Overdraft Services, 12 C.F.R. § 205.17 (2010).

has explicitly enrolled in the bank's overdraft program.[14] One of the goals of the nonenrollment default rule is to protect customers, especially low-income ones, from taking the equivalent of extraordinarily high interest loans—indeed, loans with interest rates of up to 7,000 percent. The central idea is that many people end up paying large fees essentially by inadvertence. If the default rule is switched, so that consumers end up in the program only if they really want to, then they will benefit from a safeguard against excessive charges.

In principle, the regulation should have had a very large effect, and indeed, an understanding of the power of default rules helped to motivate its promulgation. The Board explicitly observed that "studies have suggested … [that] consumers are likely to adhere to the established default rule, that is, the outcome that would apply if the consumer takes no action." The Board also referred to research on the power of automatic enrollment to increase participation in retirement savings plans.[15] It emphasized the phenomenon of unrealistic optimism, suggesting that consumers might well think, unrealistically, that they would not overdraw their accounts.[16] No one argues that a default rule can entirely cure the problem of unrealistic optimism, but it can provide a remedy against its most serious harmful effects, at least if the default is sticky.

What happened? The evidence suggests that the effect of the regulation has not been nearly as large as might have been expected. The reason is that people are opting into the program, and thus rejecting the nonenrollment default, in large numbers. The precise figures remain unclear, but the overall level of opt-in seems to be around 15 percent, and at some banks it is as high as 60 percent.

---

14. See Lauren E. Willis, *When Nudges Fail: Slippery Defaults*, 80 U. Chi. L. Rev. 1155, 1174–75 (2013) (explaining the regulation).
15. 74 Fed Reg at 59038 & n. 25.
16. 74 Fed Reg at 59044.

Here is the most striking finding: Among people who exceed the amount in their checking account more than ten times per month, the level appears to be over 50 percent.

What explains the large number of opt-ins? As Lauren Willis shows in an important and illuminating article, a central reason is that many banks dislike the regulation, want to be able to charge overdraft fees, and hence are using a number of smart strategies to facilitate opt-in.[17] As Willis demonstrates, they have taken steps to make opt-in as easy as possible—for example, simply by pushing a button on an ATM. They have also engaged in active marketing and created economic incentives to persuade people to opt in. They have cleverly exploited people's belief, which is often inaccurate, that it is costly not to be enrolled in the program. For example, they have sent materials that "explain": "You can protect yourself from...fees normally charged to you by merchants for returned items," and "The Bounce Overdraft Program was designed to protect you from the cost...of having your transactions denied." They have sent their customers a lot of material to persuade them that enrollment is in their interests.

Showing an implicit (or maybe even explicit) understanding of behavioral economics, they have enlisted loss aversion and consumer confusion to encourage account holders to think that they will lose money if they do not opt in. Here's an example: *"Don't lose your ATM and Debit Card Overdraft Protection"..."STAY PROTECTED with...ATM and Debit Card Overdraft Coverage."*[18]

Consider the following excerpt from one bank's marketing materials, explicitly exploiting loss aversion:

Yes: Keep my account working the same with Shareplus ATM and debit card overdraft coverage.

17. Willis, *supra* note 14, at 1186–87.
18. *Id.* at 1189–92.

No: Change my account to remove Shareplus ATM and debit card overdraft coverage.[19]

As one bank employee explained, "people are scared of change so they'll opt in [to overdraft] to avoid change."[20] Banks have also used social norms to encourage people to opt in, with advertisements cheerfully announcing, "The majority of our members prefer having this service."

There is a large contrast here with the retirement context, where providers enthusiastically endorse automatic enrollment and have no interest in getting people to opt out. Those who run retirement plans are quite happy if more people are participating and hence they are glad to work with employers, or the government, to promote enrollment. The Federal Reserve Board called for a default that banks dislike, and at least to some extent, the banks have had their revenge.

From this illuminating tale, Willis draws an important general lesson: If regulated institutions are strongly opposed to the default rule and have easy access to their customers, they may well be able to use a variety of strategies, including behavioral ones, to encourage people to move in their preferred directions—and thus to abandon the default. In such cases, the default is slippery not because choosers independently dislike it but because companies and firms convince them to choose to reject it. If regulators really want to protect people, they might find it necessary to take further steps to make the default rule sticky, if ensuring that it sticks is indeed the goal. In fact they might even want to impose a mandate. Hence it would be possible to ask: Shouldn't the Federal Reserve Board, now or in the near future, give serious consideration to strengthening its

---

19. *Id.* at 1192.
20. *Id.*

rule, perhaps by prohibiting, or at least severely constraining, the use of overdraft protection programs?

In the end, the answer might be yes. But policymakers should be careful before drawing such conclusions about the overdraft example, and indeed about imposing mandates in all domains where default rules tend not to stick. As we have seen, they might not stick because people just don't like them. In such cases, the fact that they are mere defaults rather than mandates might be both good and important. Any default rule might be ill-chosen, or it might not fit individual circumstances. If so, the fact that people can reject it is a valuable safeguard. In this sense, people are free by default not because they are liberated to focus on what matters to them but because they are at liberty to reject the default.

Something similar might well be said if and when self-interested institutions that are burdened by a default rule are able to convince people to reject it. The tale of the overdraft protection seems to be one of regulatory failure (as Willis herself takes it) or at least incomplete success, but things are not so clear. Recall that a lot of people (perhaps as high as 85 percent) do not opt in to the program. Recall, too, that the largest proportion of people who opt in are those who actually go over their checking limits. For such people, it is not implausible to think that opt-in is a good idea. At least some of them might well be rational to opt in. If they cannot borrow from their bank—and overdraft protection is a form of borrowing—they might have to borrow from someone else, which would mean a level of inconvenience and high (and at least potentially even higher) interest rates. If so, many people might have to resort to payday lenders, whose rates may or may not be lower.

Because such inconvenience can be a real problem and because higher rates can hit people especially hard, overdraft protection might well be in the interest of many or most of the people who end up opting in. Note in this regard that when states have regulated payday lenders, consumers have resorted to almost equally expensive sources of money (such as pawn shops).[21] This finding strongly suggests that if people cannot have access to overdraft protection, they may simply go elsewhere.

With this point in mind, the Federal Reserve's policy might even be deemed a significant success. People are no longer automatically enrolled in overdraft protection, and the vast majority of customers no longer have such protection, which may well be saving them money. At the same time, those who want such protection or need it have signed up for it. That sounds pretty good. What's the problem?

The answer might be that many of those who are enrolled in the system and are receiving that protection are worse off as a result. Perhaps they do not understand the program and its costs. Perhaps they are at risk of bouncing checks not because they need a loan but because they haven't focused on their bank accounts and whether they are about to go over. To evaluate the existing situation, we would need to know a lot more about the population who opt in. Perhaps they are insufficiently informed or attentive.

If so, there is a good argument that further steps should be taken, perhaps in the form of email or text reminders. Compare the idea of "bill shock," which occurs when people find that they have gone over their cell phone limits and have a surprisingly big bill at the end of the month. In 2010, the Federal Communications Commission proposed a rule to require providers to notify consumers, by text message, that they were going to exceed their minutes. The providers responded by agreeing to provide such notification voluntarily. In the context of bank overdraft protection, the current default rules, combined with some smart nudges, would likely be preferable to any kind of mandate or ban.

21. *See* Tatiana Homonoff, *Essays in Behavioral Economics and Public Policy* (Sept. 2013) (unpublished Ph.D. dissertation, Princeton University), *available at* http://arks .princeton.edu/ark:/88435/dsp01jw827b79g.

ALTERING RULES AND FRAMING RULES

The overdraft example demonstrates the importance of focusing not only on default rules but also on two other kinds: altering rules and framing rules.[22]

Altering rules establish *how people can change the default.* Choice architects might say that consumers can opt in or opt out by making an easy phone call (good) or by sending a quick email (even better). Alternatively, choice architects, confident that the default is right for most people, might increase the costs of departing from it. For example, they might require people to fill out complex forms or impose a cooling-off period. They might also say that even if people make a change, the outcome will "revert" to the default after a certain period (say, a year), requiring repeated steps (a "reverting default rule"). Or they might require some form of education or training, insisting on a measure of learning before people depart from the default.

Framing rules establish and regulate the kinds of "frames" that people can use when they try to convince people to opt in or opt out. As Willis shows, financial institutions enlisted loss aversion in support of opt-in. They were smart to do so. Behaviorally informed strategies of this kind could turn out to be highly effective. But that is a potential problem. Even if they are not technically deceptive, they might count as manipulative. Those who believe in freedom of choice and seek to avoid manipulation might want to constrain the permissible set of frames—subject, of course, to existing safeguards for freedom of speech. Framing rules might be used to reduce the risk of manipulation.

22. *See* Willis, *supra* note 14, for an excellent discussion.

Consider an analogy. If a company says that its product is "90 percent fat-free," people are likely to be drawn to it, far more so than if the company says that its product is "10 percent fat." The two phrases mean the same thing, and the "90 percent fat-free" frame is legitimately seen as a form of manipulation. In 2011, the American government allowed companies to say that their products are 90 percent fat-free—but only if they also say that they are 10 percent fat. We could imagine similar constraints on misleading or manipulative frames that are aimed to get people to opt out of the default.

To the extent that choice architects are in the business of choosing among altering rules and framing rules, they can take steps to make default rules more likely to stick, even if they do not impose mandates. They might conclude that mandates and prohibitions would be a terrible idea, but that it makes sense to make it harder for people to depart from default rules. Sometimes that is the right conclusion. The problem is that when choice architects move in this direction, they lose some of the advantages of default rules, which have the virtue of easy reversibility, at least in principle. If the altering rules are made sufficiently onerous, the default rule might not be all that different from a mandate. In societies that respect freedom, choice architects should have to be quite confident about their judgment to move in this direction.

PART II

MORALITY AND POLITICS

[3]

INFORMED CHOOSERS AND BAD DEFAULTS

Thus far we have seen that defaults often stick, but that in identifiable contexts, people will choose to choose and hence opt out. When people have strong preferences, the default rule might not matter. And when an institution that is subject to the default rule thinks that it is a bad idea, it might be able to take steps to convince people to reject it. Drawing on the underlying research, both governments and the private sector are becoming far more sophisticated in using default rules to promote their preferred outcomes—sometimes for excellent reasons, sometimes out of self-interest.

We have also seen that in many domains, choice architects can achieve desirable goals, while maintaining freedom of choice and at low cost, by selecting sensible default rules and avoiding harmful ones. But which default rule should choice architects select? How do we know which is sensible and which is harmful? What are the relevant moral considerations?

Most of my focus here is on choice architects who work for the public sector, in the capacity of legislators, regulators, or judges. Selection of default rules by the private sector raises different questions. But many of the conclusions bear on the choices of private actors as well. In a well-functioning market, of course, competitive pressures should lead to optimal default rules if choice architects are attempting to maximize profits. If companies select default rules that harm consumers, they should soon find themselves with fewer consumers.

Under optimistic assumptions, the profit motive should therefore be sufficient to produce good default rules; armed with an understanding of when and why default rules stick, companies should act consistently with that motive. Invisible hand mechanisms ought to work.[1] On the other hand, competitive pressures may, under plausible assumptions, lead to harmful rather than helpful default rules, at least in markets in which consumers are not paying a lot of attention or the harmful effects of harmful defaults are not readily visible.[2] In credit markets, and in others where the underlying product is complex and multifaceted, competitive pressures are unlikely to provide perfect solutions to the problem of bad defaults.

INFORMED CHOOSERS

There are many different answers to the question of how to select default rules.[3] Some people believe that policymakers should choose default rules that are most fair or just, or that are respectful of people's autonomy, agency, or dignity. Others think that the preferred approach should promote economic efficiency. Still others

1. For a superb discussion, see Edna Ullmann-Margalit, *The Invisible Hand and the Cunning of Reason*, 64 Soc. Res. 181 (1997).
2. *See* Oren Bar-Gill, Seduction by Contract: Law, Economics and Psychology in Consumer Markets 6–8 (2012) (exploring behavioral market failures). In addition, some companies pursue social welfare goals that do not involve maximizing profits, which may bear on their selection of default rules.
3. *See, e.g.,* Matthew D. Adler, Well-Being and Fair Distribution: Beyond Cost-Benefit Analysis 1–11 (2012) (introducing social welfare functions (SWFs) and arguing that the SWF approach should be used to evaluate governmental or other large-scale choices).

believe that choice architects should select rules that will maximize social welfare or promote social utility. Economists, welfarists, and utilitarians may not be in complete agreement, and all of them may differ from people who emphasize the importance of justice and fairness. The resulting debates may be lengthy and intractable, at least if people argue at a high level of abstraction.

The central idea. Let us begin with the standard case in which there are no (or modest) third-party effects: In such cases, the choosers are affected, but no one else is. I propose that we might bracket the deepest questions, put high theory to one side, and seek to obtain an *incompletely theorized agreement* on a preferred approach. An incompletely theorized agreement is one that can attract support from many diverse people—including those with different foundational commitments and those who are not sure which commitments they believe are foundational.[4] The basic idea is that sometimes we can make progress best, or perhaps only, by bracketing the largest and most abstract questions and seeing if we can settle on an approach that does not depend on resolving those questions.

Accepting that idea, here is the preferred approach: *Select the default rule that reflects what most people would choose if they were adequately informed.*[5] Call this the *informed-chooser approach.* Its advantage is that it should simultaneously appeal, at least in general, to those who focus on diverse values, including justice, fairness, efficiency, utility, dignity, or autonomy. If a particular default

---

4. *See* Cass R. Sunstein, Legal Reasoning and Political Conflict 35 (1996) (exploring incompletely theorized agreements as a way to achieve consensus on outcomes amid theoretical divisions).

5. *See* N. Craig Smith et al., *Smart Defaults: From Hidden Persuaders to Adaptive Helpers* 15–16 (INSEAD, Working Paper No. 2009/03/ISIC, 2009), *available at* https://flora .insead.edu/fichiersti_wp/inseadwp2009/2009-03.pdf (noting that the greatest number benefit when the "default is set to the preference most people would make when faced with making an active choice").

rule would place people in the situation that informed people would bargain their way to or select, there is good reason, whatever our foundational values, to choose that default rule—with the understanding that those who differ from the majority may opt out.

To see the appeal of the informed-chooser approach, suppose that 80 percent of people, given a great deal of information, would choose green energy. That is a strong reason to favor automatic enrollment in green energy. One reason is that if informed people would select a particular option, defaulting people into that option is respectful of their autonomy and their dignity. Another reason is that the informed-chooser approach is likely to promote people's welfare. It is also easy to defend on grounds of both efficiency and fairness. It is efficient to let people end up with what they want, and it is also fair and just.

Questions. To be sure, the informed-chooser approach raises questions. First, choice architects may not have enough information to know which approach the majority of informed people would choose. It might well be necessary for choice architects to do a great deal of empirical work in order to identify that approach. Their lack of information is a point in favor of active choosing. If choice architects lack the knowledge that would enable them to select the appropriate default, they might want to ask people to choose.

Second, the idea of "informed" choice will sometimes raise hard conceptual problems. Exactly what does it mean to be informed? Is the idea limited to factual knowledge? As behavioral scientists have stressed, people may blunder even if they have full access to the facts. Recall that they may display unrealistic optimism or discount the long term ("present bias"). Even if they are made aware of statistical realities, their judgments about probability may go wrong. Perhaps those who make such errors can be counted as insufficiently informed, but this claim is a bit of a cheat; people may err even if they have all relevant information. If informed people are subject to biases, choice architects may not want to base default rules on their choices. They may want to correct biases rather than cater to them. Perhaps the idealized chooser should be unbiased, not just informed.

At the same time, there is a serious risk in any effort to develop the idea of an informed chooser by attempting to correct behavioral biases. The risk is that choice architects will not really be deciding what choosers want but will instead be relying on what they believe to be right—in which case the choosers, as agents, do not seem particularly important. To avoid that risk, choice architects should probably rely on what informed choosers actually do, while acknowledging that if their choices can really be shown to be opposed to their interests (perhaps because of a behavioral bias), then it might make sense to depart from those choices in order to protect people's welfare. In this area, the presumption should be in favor of allowing (factually informed) choosers to do as they wish.

Third, people who are concerned with fairness or distribution may fear that the bargaining power of the stronger side will cause informed people on the weaker side to have to settle on an unfair agreement, with a default rule that hurts them, and that a fairer default would be better. At least in a contractual situation, the stronger side might be able to extract especially favorable terms. That is indeed a problem. For those who are concerned about it, the challenge is that if regulators block the exchange, on the ground that it is unfair, disadvantaged people might turn out to be the real losers. For example, if the government requires employers to provide workers with "for cause" protection against discharge, some people might not be hired in the first place, and wages and benefits might go down. It is true that in a bargaining situation, the informed-chooser approach might lead to harsh results, and it is possible that those results should be prevented—but the empirical question is whether the cure is worse than the disease, in the sense that it might hurt the very people it is intended to help.

Fourth, it is important to emphasize that in a setting that involves bargaining and negotiation, it might be especially difficult to know what informed people would choose. A default rule that seems to favor one side may not be the provision to which informed people would bargain. For example, it is tempting to think that workers would want "good cause" protection against being discharged, which would mean that employers would not be allowed to fire them at will. But perhaps workers do not really need that protection; perhaps employers do not really fire workers arbitrarily, or do not do so very often, even if the law allows it. Perhaps workers would end up with some kind of salary cut if they received "good cause" protection.

Informed workers and informed employers might not bargain their way toward a "good cause" provision for the termination of employment if the consequence of that provision would be to impose high costs on employers (and eventually on employees) without providing important or meaningful safeguards for workers. So, too, informed customers and energy companies might refuse to bargain their way to a particular "green" default if it turns out to impose much higher costs. (Of course, the existence of third-party effects may argue in favor of green defaults.)

On all of these counts, actual evidence—about what informed choosers do—can be extremely important. In many contexts, it should be possible to obtain that evidence. For example, people might simply be provided with information, and policymakers might see what they decide. Policymakers might conduct pilot programs in which people are given relevant materials and then choose. Indeed, selection of a default rule might well be preceded by a period of active choosing, undertaken as a way of assembling information about what informed choosers in fact select. And if experts are justifiably confident about their selection, their own judgments may suffice; the right portfolio for retirement savings is an arguable example, at least if the experts really know what would be best for most people.

Policymakers might also want to obtain information about the level of opt-out under various alternatives. If the opt-out rate is low, the default rule might be pretty good. Perhaps experiments would provide such information. If only 12 percent of people opt out under A and 50 percent opt out under B, we have reason to believe that A is better.

Of course, majority rule can be too crude. Suppose that there are two potential default rules, A and B. Suppose that 55 percent of informed people would be largely indifferent between A and B but would slightly prefer A. Suppose, too, that because of their unusual situation, 45 percent of people would strongly prefer B. At first glance, policymakers should probably select B, because almost half of the population would very much like it and the (narrow) majority would care only a little. The example shows that it is important to ask not only about which approach would be preferred by informed people but also about the intensity of their preferences.

Intensity and opt-out. There is an important qualification. It is clear that if people have intense preferences, they are more likely to opt out. It follows that policymakers might not want those with intense preferences to provide the justification for setting the default rule—because, for them, that rule will not stick in any case, and so will not matter. Clear and intense contrary preferences are the essential reason that default rules do not stick—and for those with weak preferences, such rules will stick even if they would not prefer it.

For this reason, it would be reasonable to use majority rule, even or perhaps especially, in the face of strong contrary preferences. But this suggestion raises a further question: In the particular context, is there good reason for confidence that those with strong preferences will switch? They might not do so if for them, inertia is a powerful force, or if any kind of effort tax proves decisive, or if their otherwise strong preferences are affected by the suggestion implicit in the default rule.

The most natural way to think of the choice is in terms of costs and benefits. If a default rule turned out to stick, what would be the costs and what would be the benefits? (Importantly, the informed-chooser approach is a simple way of answering the cost-benefit question; in general, the approach that informed choosers want is the approach that has net benefits.) Distributional issues may of course matter as well. Who is being helped and who is being hurt? In the example just given, there is a good argument that default rule B would be best because it gives people who care the rule they want and because those who get the rule they don't want do not much care. It is easy to imagine cases in which the choice architect would seek "tailored" or personalized default rules, suitable to particular people and settings (see part III). It is also easy to imagine circum-stances in which the choice among possible default rules is hard, so that active choosing is better (see chapter 4).

Discrimination and social norms. The question of marital names suggests an interesting qualification to the idea that the default rule should track the choices of informed people. Taken seriously, that idea suggests that states should presume that men want to keep their premarital surnames and women want to change their surnames to those of their husbands. But a default rule of this kind would be discriminatory and would almost certainly be found unconstitutional.[6]

---

6. *See* Elizabeth F. Emens, *Changing Name Changing: Framing Rules and the Future of Marital Names*, 74 U. Chi. L. Rev. 761, 834–36 (2007) (discussing how setting legal defaults that differ for men and women would raise constitutional problems).

The example shows that in some settings, informed choices lack authority if they run afoul of important social commitments, at least if government proposes to use those choices as a basis for policy.[7] In the context of marital names, the theory must be that even if men and women behave differently, governments cannot simply track their behavior, because they should not entrench discriminatory norms. Entrenchment of those norms is a form of favoritism, not neutrality. It is illegitimate because it honors and perpetuates discriminatory practices, in part because it likely affects people's preferences and values. Law has an expressive function, and what it expresses might turn out to matter.

Distributional questions again, and many informed choosers. The discussion thus far has generally assumed that choosers are not much different from one another, or that they can be sorted into just a few groups, so that if policymakers know what some informed choosers would do, they know what many or most would do. Of course that assumption is artificial. Sometimes the class of choosers includes many subgroups. Informed choosers who are poor but in good health might want a health insurance plan that is inexpensive and suits people who are healthy. Informed choosers who are wealthy and who face serious health risks might want a quite different health insurance plan. With respect to privacy, informed choosers do not make the same judgments, because their situations and values diverge. With respect to retirement savings, some people need a lot of money now and will not want the same plan as people who have no such need.

In the face of diversity, policymakers might opt for active choosing, on the ground that a unitary approach, based on the idea of an

---

7. The domain of marital names overlaps in this regard with that of racially based adoption policies. *See* R. Richard Banks, *The Color of Desire: Fulfilling Adoptive Parents' Racial Preferences Through Discriminatory State Action*, 107 YALE L.J. 875, 877–82 (1998) (discussing deeply divided views over "race matching" in adoptions).

informed chooser, is simply too crude. Alternatively, they might want personalized defaults, recognizing the diversity of informed choosers. I will explore both possibilities in detail. For now, I shall continue with the assumption that an informed-chooser approach will work well enough, acknowledging that the assumption is sometimes artificial.

PENALTY DEFAULTS

Suppose that choice architects do not know which rule would be chosen by informed people. If not, standard contract theory suggests that they might favor what is called a "penalty default," which is designed to elicit just that information.[8] Under this approach, the law, or the choice architect, would place the burden of making a change on the party who is most likely to seek change. Instead of tracking people's informed choices, this approach attempts to figure out what those choices actually are—by using a default rule that penalizes people who do not explicitly reveal those choices.

For example, employees sometimes lack information about their legal rights, displaying unrealistic optimism.[9] They think that they have certain rights, such as the right not to be fired except "for cause," even though they do not. In these circumstances, a default rule that gives certain rights to employees, and forces employers to try to convince employees to give up those rights, might increase the

---

8. *See* Ian Ayres & Robert Gertner, *Filling Gaps in Incomplete Contracts: An Economic Theory of Default Rules*, 99 YALE L.J. 87, 91–95 (1989) (explaining that penalty defaults reveal information and providing ways to analyze the efficiency of penalty defaults).

9. *See* RICHARD B. FREEMAN & JOEL ROGERS, WHAT WORKERS WANT 118–22 (1999) (finding, in a survey of individuals in the workforce, that these individuals frequently overstated the protections available in the workplace).

flow of information between the parties and to the legal system.[10] It might ensure that workers learn what their rights really are.

Suppose that if the default rule confers certain rights on employees—say, to job security—employers will want to "buy" those rights. If this is the case, significant information will be disclosed to employees, simply as part of the process by which employers bargain. A default rule that protects workers might give them important information when they would otherwise overestimate their legal rights. Of course it is possible that the information will be in small print or at the final stage of a job negotiation, in which case it will not be so helpful. But perhaps the legal system could require actual, rather than merely formal, knowledge. Understanding one's actual rights is exceedingly important.

The broader lesson should be clear. If policymakers know what people's informed preferences are, they should usually build a default rule on the basis of that knowledge. But if they do not know what people's informed preferences are, they might choose a default rule because it increases the likelihood that important information will be revealed to people who lack that information. Such a default can ensure that people will end up knowing about their rights— and choose accordingly.

THIRD PARTIES

If there are third-party effects, of course the assessment of default rules will be affected. The issue is no longer limited to the welfare of choosers.

10. *See* Samuel Issacharoff, *Contracting for Employment: The Limited Return of the Common Law*, 74 Tex. L. Rev. 1783, 1792–94 (1996) (arguing for penalty default rules that would increase information sharing).

Suppose that under default rule *A*, significant costs are imposed on third parties, but that under default rule *B* those costs are avoided. If so, *B* is likely to be preferable by far. In the case of default rules for organ donations and energy, this possibility is far from hypothetical. A default rule in favor of organ donation would of course produce significant benefits for third parties. The reason for presumed consent is not to protect choosers but to protect the people who would benefit from an increase in the number of available organs. Similarly, some energy choices would impose lower environmental and other costs; green defaults might be justifiable on that ground.

In such cases, there is a strong argument for preferring the default rule that reduces those costs. The selection of the default rule should be based on an analysis of all relevant benefits and costs (capaciously understood to include factors that are hard or impossible to quantify). Choice architects should select the approach that maximizes net benefits, understood to include the full range of ingredients in social welfare. (Of course distributional considerations might matter as well.) And if third-party effects are large, mere default rules might not be enough. If a particular approach prevents the imposition of serious costs on third parties, then there is a good argument that it should be a mandate, not subject to opt-out. But in some cases, the existence and magnitude of third-party effects are disputed, and in such cases the best approach might be a default rule that prevents such effects.

True, it may not be easy to identify the default that would maximize net benefits. In the case of energy providers, for example, choice architects should have to consider not only the costs of service but also environmental costs, including the costs of greenhouse gas emissions, which would require assessment of the social cost of carbon (meant to capture the monetary value of a ton of carbon emissions). The overall assessment may present formidable challenges. Unlike in cases where the only question is the welfare of choosers, moreover, active choosing would not be a way out of the dilemma, because it would likely result in disregard of the interests of third parties. Choice architects cannot afford to ignore those interests. They must do the best they can to choose default rules that reflect them, even as they acknowledge the possibility that their choice might be wrong.

This argument can be generalized. In every case, the question is which approach produces the highest net benefits, broadly understood (and acknowledging that distributional considerations might matter, posing a potential choice between aggregate welfare and fair distribution). The informed-chooser approach follows from the focus on maximizing net benefits. If choice architects should select the default that informed choosers would like, it is because that approach produces the highest net benefits.

BAD DEFAULTS

Default rules can be badly chosen or misused by private and public institutions alike. In fact, some such rules can be extremely harmful. Imagine a voting system that says that if you do nothing, your vote will be registered as favoring the incumbent—but you can opt out if you like. Or imagine a nation that defaults you into a certain political party or religion—but allows you to opt out. Or a rental car company that defaults you into all sorts of insurance policies and extras that are essentially a waste of money—but allows you to opt out.

I have noted that market forces constrain at least some of the most harmful default rules. Competitive markets impose real limits on bad defaults. Before long, customers are not likely to have much interest in companies that choose a series of such defaults. For this reason, many companies choose default rules that are helpful rather than harmful; for example, the default settings for computers and cell phones are generally in the interest of customers.

As also noted, however, companies may have an incentive to promote defaults that are helpful to them but harmful to their customers, especially when those defaults can be put in fine print and when the relevant attributes of the product are shrouded and not salient. Recall the problem of automatic enrollment in overdraft "protection." In credit markets, financial institutions may be helped, not punished, if they exploit behavioral biases such as unrealistic optimism; providers who do not exploit those biases may find themselves at a competitive disadvantage.

Serious problems may also arise when there are information asymmetries between sellers and buyers, or when choice architects can help construct consumers' preferences. For example, a company may know exactly what it wants, but consumers may not know what they want, and so there may be opportunities for companies to come up with deals, including defaults, that are bad from the standpoint of consumers. Enrollment in overdraft programs is an example here as well. Another example is the idea of default enrollment in warranty programs for (say) cell phones or tablets. For many people, such programs are a waste of money—a form of insurance that just is not worth the cost. Those who sell warranties often know what they are doing, and default purchases, or even sincere suggestions, can lead people in bad directions.

Consider in this regard the practice of "negative-option marketing." This practice occurs when people who accept a "free" product are automatically enrolled in a plan or program that carries a monthly fee (unless they explicitly opt out).[11] Customers might, for example,

---

11. *See* 16 C.F.R. § 425.1 (2012) (regulating the use of prenotification negative-option plans); FTC, NEGATIVE OPTIONS 2 (2009), *available at* http://www.ftc.gov/

receive a hotel room for free, which is nice, but as a result they might find themselves enrolled in a program that charges them a nontrivial sum per month. The monthly charge might be mentioned quietly and obscurely, if at all, and if it is mentioned people might be given (quietly) the option to opt out. Alternatively, people might be sent some kind of gift and be told that unless they return it, they will be enrolled in a program of some kind, for which they have to pay.

In some cases, negative-option marketing has an unfortunate effect: It exploits people's tendency toward inertia in a way that can cost them a great deal of money. Customers might not always look at the details of their monthly credit card statement, and if they see the relevant item they might assume that all is well, and they might not cancel the plan until they have (automatically) paid a great deal. In this case, inertia, and apparently a kind of "effort tax," are working against customers' interests, and companies are aware of that fact. In the United States, the Federal Trade Commission has expressed serious concerns about this kind of marketing, and some states have required clear disclosure, so that people do not get fooled.[12]

I received a little lesson about this general problem when American Express graciously offered to provide me with a free three-month subscription to several magazines of my choice. As a result, I found myself automatically subscribing to those magazines, even though I didn't like them, at full price—for well over a decade after the three-month period. It was not until I faced the prospect of government employment and the resulting salary cut that I canceled my subscriptions. (It wasn't that easy.)

There are both private and public analogues. Inertia, endorsement, and loss aversion might ensure that default rules stick even

os/2009/02/P064202negativeoptionreport.pdf (describing four types of plans that could be classified as negative-option marketing).

12. *See* FTC, *supra* note 11, at 5 (discussing the various problems posed by negative-option marketing).

if they are not in people's interests. Consider, for example, a default rule that automatically enrolls people in a health insurance plan that is a bad deal for their circumstances, or one that signs them up for an exercise plan that they do not need, do not use, and perhaps hate. Automatic enrollment can be a waste or even a disaster.

For reasons discussed earlier, the risk should not be overstated. We have seen that extreme defaults do not stick when people have preferences that are independent of the default rule and are willing to expend effort to set things right. Nonetheless, harmful defaults impose significant burdens and costs, not least because inertia may not be so easy to overcome, and because many consumers may think that defaults were chosen for a good and legitimate reason. Recall in particular that low-income people are, in certain circumstances at least, especially unlikely to opt out—a finding that suggests that default rules may prove especially harmful to people who can least afford to be harmed.

Let's take stock. In this chapter, my central argument has been that when setting default rules, choice architects should ask what informed choosers would decide. If they focus on informed choosers, they can promote, at once, welfare, efficiency, autonomy, and fairness. A difficult question is how much content is given to the idea of the informed chooser; does the idea refer to information as such, or does it also call for correction of behavioral biases? When third parties are at risk, the analysis must be broadened, because the default rule will affect a wide range of people whose interests must be taken into account, raising the possible need to attend to distributional considerations. I have also emphasized that default rules carry risks. If automatic enrollment is not made clear and transparent to those who are enrolled, it can be considered a form of manipulation. The problem is worse if it is not in people's long-term interest.

[4]

EMBRACING CHOICE

In the liberal tradition, many people strongly endorse active choosing. With his emphasis on welfare and self-development, John Stuart Mill was certainly enthusiastic about the idea. In a free society, both public officials and private citizens might want to insist that the presumption should be in favor of active choosing, not merely freedom of choice.

There is an affirmative case for active choosing: People exercise their liberty through choice-making, and as they make choices, they learn, develop their capacities, and become more free. There is also a negative case for active choosing: Those who greatly distrust private or public institutions, and want to avoid any kind of steering by them, will have considerable interest in active choices. They will reject default rules of any kind and put the key questions to people themselves. This approach has special advantages in the face of diversity—especially if default rules would otherwise be impersonal.

Note that active choosing comes in two varieties: optional and required. When people visit a grocery store or shop for cell phones or sneakers, they may make active choices, but they can leave the store immediately without any kind of adverse effect; no punishment is imposed if they fail to make a selection. So, too, active choosing can be "prompted"—as when people are asked whether they want to become organ donors when they renew their driver's licenses, or when they are asked on their tax form whether they want to give money to help finance political campaigns. In such cases, the questions can be ignored. If, by contrast, people are told that they cannot receive a driver's license without saying whether they want to be organ donors, an active choice is essentially required. Admittedly, the line between optional and required active choosing is not entirely clear, and I will revisit it shortly; in all cases, something happens if one does not make an active choice (for example, no groceries and no cell phone). My major focus here is on required active choosing, though I will discuss the optional variety as well.

LIFE WITHOUT DEFAULTS?

With required active choosing, people must make an actual decision among the various options; they are not defaulted into any particular alternative. A small example: A website or an app might ask you: Do you want to receive notifications? If choice is required, you can't move on unless you answer. In taxicabs in New York, you are asked whether you want a receipt; you can say yes or no. What is requested, though not required, is an active choice. (Note, however, that if you don't indicate your preferences, you don't get a receipt.)

With respect to health care, privacy, organ donation, and savings, choice architects might reject both opt-out and opt-in and simply require (or ask) people to indicate their preferences. It is important to emphasize the potential advantages of active choosing in nations and cultures in which certain issues (such as organ donation) are highly sensitive, and in which people would greatly resist the idea of being defaulted into outcomes that they might believe to be intrusive or offensive. In cases of this kind, default rules might run into fierce resistance, and active choosing might seem much better.

The possibility of cultural differences should be underlined. In some societies, a default rule (say, that you enter into an arranged marriage, until you take certain steps to opt out, and indeed opt-out may not be allowed) is acceptable, whereas active choosing is not. In other cultures, active choosing is so unambiguously the norm that any effort to create default rules would seem an unacceptable intrusion on liberty, welfare, or both. Of course cultures are not static. Some of the most interesting social movements involve a shift from active choosing to default rules or vice versa.[1] (Research on when and how such shifts occur would be highly illuminating; note that social norms might also operate as the equivalent of defaults.)[2] The major point is that some default rules run up against strong cultural norms in favor of active choosing, and in such cases defaults are not feasible.

I shall have a great deal to say in support of active choosing, but note three important complications at the outset. First, what does it mean to "require" people to indicate their preferences? Those who insist on the inevitability of default rules will object that there is no good answer to this question. Even if choice architects seek to promote active choosing, they have to specify what happens if *people simply refuse to choose.* An apparently triumphant question: Isn't the answer some kind of default rule?

The question is a good one, because some kind of default rule is ultimately necessary. In ordinary consumer markets, the answer is straightforward: You don't get a good or a service unless you make some kind of active choice. The default rule is nonownership. Something similar is true in politics, where you don't vote unless

---

1. For relevant discussion, see Edna Ullmann-Margalit, *Revision of Norms*, 100 ETHICS 756 (1990).
2. *See* Young Eun Huh et al., *Social Defaults: Observed Choices Become Choice Defaults*, 41 J. CONS. RES. 746 (2014).

you express a choice, and in social life, where you are not a member of certain associations, or even lack friends, unless you make relevant choices. For much of the territory, the straightforward answer is perfectly sufficient. The answer certainly works in cases of prompted choice, where silence means that you don't engage in the relevant action (making a doctor's appointment, taking one's medicine), or enroll or participate in the relevant program. But in some cases, things are a bit more complicated. The basic claim of those who insist on required active choosing is that choice architects should call for it *through a sanction that is so severe that it is the functional equivalent of a mandate.* People are required to make an active choice in the sense that if they do not, they will lose, or will not obtain, something they really want or need.

For example, a state might say that unless people indicate whether they want to be organ donors, they cannot receive their driver's licenses. Or an employer might say that until employees choose a retirement plan or a health insurance plan, they cannot begin to work. Or a website operator might say that until you indicate your preferences with respect to privacy or further notifications, you can't proceed to the site. It remains true that people can simply refuse, in which case a default rule does apply (nonenrollment or nonuse). But this point need not greatly disturb those who believe in active choosing; they should happily concede it.

We have already seen the second complication, which is that some people prefer not to choose. In that sense, it can be paternalistic to insist on active choosing. I explore this point in some detail in chapter 5.

The third complication is that while active choosing is designed to elicit people's preferences and to do so in a neutral fashion, the very decision to require active choosing might contain a "signal," and that signal might affect choosers. Suppose, for example, that the default rule has been nonenrollment in an organ donation plan, and that in order to promote organ donation, a state shifts to active choosing. We can imagine three potential outcomes. First, people might be genuinely unaffected by the signal. Second, the shift might be taken to signal the state's view that organ donation is a good idea—hence the organ donation rate might increase because people receive, and trust, that signal. Third, the signal might be taken to signal the state's view that organ donation is a good idea, and people might receive, and distrust, that signal, thus reducing participation below the level obtained with a nonenrollment default. (Such a response might be a form of "reactance.") Any of these three outcomes is possible, depending on the strength of the signal and people's reactions to it.

Notwithstanding these points, inertia greatly matters, and it is reasonable to speculate that *active choosing would usually produce higher participation rates than an opt-in system but lower rates than an opt-out system.* The speculation is generally supported by what is currently known. For example, active choosing has been found to produce far higher levels of savings than default rules that require people to opt in (but lower than in the case of automatic enrollment).[3] Or return to the question of privacy. Most web browsers currently default people into a situation in which their movements are visible and can be tracked. Another possibility would be to ask customers—either the first time they open the browser or periodically—about the privacy setting they prefer, and perhaps prevent them from proceeding until they answer. A reasonable guess is that this approach would produce more privacy than

---

3. *See* Gabriel D. Carroll et al., *Optimal Defaults and Active Decisions*, 124 Q.J. ECON. 1639, 1670 (2009) (describing the results of the 401(k) experiment testing active choice). *But see* Judd Kessler & Alvin Roth, *Don't Take "No" for an Answer: An Experiment with Actual Organ Donor Registrations* (Nat'l Bureau of Econ. Research, Working Paper No. 20378, 2014) (finding that prompted choice produces higher levels of organ donation than required active choosing).

they currently enjoy.[4] The choice between prompted choice and required choice also raises empirical questions, with some evidence suggesting that required choice can actually produce lower participation rates.[5]

CHOOSING, ACTIVE BUT INFLUENCED

It is also possible to imagine a host of variations on active choosing. We can identify a continuum of approaches, from the most neutral form of active choosing to forms that choice architects self-consciously devise in an attempt to influence what people decide.

For example, active choosing might be "enhanced," or influenced, in the sense that one of the choices might be highlighted or favored, perhaps through the use of behaviorally informed strategies.[6] If choice architects intend to avoid a default rule but nonetheless want to promote selection of one of the options, they might put it at the top of a list, or use a bold or large font, or adopt verbal descriptions that are especially salient or appealing. It may well be possible for choice architects to frame the choices in a way that inclines people to select what the architects want.

---

4. Whether that would be desirable is, of course, another question. Recall that information is a public good and individually rational decisions in favor of protecting privacy might produce less information than is desirable. *See* Eric Johnson et al., *Defaults, Framing and Privacy: Why Opting In–Opting Out,* 13 MARKETING LETTERS 5 (2002). For some empirical complications, see Lauren E. Willis, *Why Not Privacy by Default?,* 29 BERKELEY TECH. L.J. 61 (2014).

5. *See* Kessler & Roth, *supra* note 3.

6. *See* Punam Anand Keller et al., *Enhanced Active Choice: A New Method to Motivate Behavior Change,* 21 J. CONSUMER PSYCHOL. 376, 378 (2011) (arguing that "enhanced active choice," which communicates the preferred choice by highlighting the losses incumbent in the nonpreferred alternative, will result in more compliance than "basic active choice").

In one study, choice was "enhanced" by enlisting loss aversion to discourage selection of the option disfavored by the experimenters. The experimenters introduced several different messages this way:

> We would like you to imagine that you are interested in protecting your health. The Center [sic] for Disease Control indicates that a flu shot significantly reduces the risk of getting or passing on the flu virus. Your employer tells you about a hypothetical program that recommends you get a flu shot this Fall and possibly save $50 off your bi-weekly or monthly health insurance contribution cost.[7]

In the *opt-in condition*, people were asked to "Place a check in the box if you will get a Flu shot this Fall." In a "neutral active-choice condition," people were asked to "Place a check in one box: I will get a flu shot this Fall or, I will not get a flu shot this Fall." With "enhanced or influenced choice," people were asked to choose between two alternatives: "I will get a Flu Shot this Fall to reduce my risk of getting the flu and I want to save $50" or "I will not get a Flu Shot this Fall even if it means I may increase my risk of getting the flu and I don't want to save $50." It is obvious that the enhanced choice condition enlisted loss aversion ("even if it means"). Compared to the opt-in condition, the active-choice condition led to a significant increase in the percentage of people who would get a flu shot; notably, the percentage was highest when active choice was influenced or enhanced.

There is an obvious parallel here with the efforts of banks to promote opt-in by enlisting loss aversion and other behaviorally informed strategies. The principal point is that active choosing can be more or less neutral with respect to the relevant options. As the choice

7. *Id.* at 379.

architect becomes decreasingly neutral, active choosing starts to look closer to a default rule.

ACTIVE CHOOSING AND NOT CHOOSING

What might be said on behalf of active choosing? For those who prize freedom, the answer is fairly clear if the antonym is a mandate or a ban (see chapter 8). But suppose that the alternative is a default rule, which maintains freedom of choice. Why is active choosing better than that?[8]

One answer is that unless people have actually said that they want some good or service, we cannot be sure what they want. On this view, active choosing is a valuable safeguard against bad outcomes, resulting from mistaken judgments about what people really want and what it is in their interest to have. If, for example, a cell phone store presumes that certain consumers want certain phones and defaults them into ownership (subject to opt-out), there would be an undue risk that people would end up with phones that they do not want. Requiring active choosing in ordinary markets minimizes the costs of error, and in that sense makes people's lives better. Consider Friedrich Hayek's claim that "the awareness of our irremediable ignorance of most of what is known to somebody [who is a planner] is *the chief basis of the argument for liberty.*"[9]

---

8. A growing literature explores, or has implications for, the topic of active choosing. *See* Bruce Carlin et al., Libertarian Paternalism, Information Sharing, and Financial Decision-Making 5 (Mar. 12, 2013) (unpublished manuscript), *available at* http://faculty.haas.berkeley.edu/manso/liberty.pdf (arguing for a judicious use of libertarian paternalism so as not to stifle social learning and the development of self-corrective behavior).

9. Friedrich Hayek, *The Market and Other Orders*, in THE COLLECTED WORKS OF F. A. HAYEK 384 (Bruce Caldwell ed., 2013).

One understanding of Hayek's suggestion, with the reference to liberty, is that active choosing is necessary to protect people's autonomy, not their welfare. Perhaps people have a right to make their own choices, whatever the results of those choices. Some people embrace a form of what philosophers call *liberal perfectionism*; they believe that societies, and governments, should inculcate particular characteristics, including energy, initiative, authenticity, and a capacity for agency.[10] If you endorse perfectionism, you might well favor active choosing on autonomy grounds. And if so, you might also think that without some affirmative statement of intention, free people should not find themselves forced (or assumed to want) goods or services. But an account that is based on people's welfare rather than their autonomy seems especially straightforward, and I think that it is what Hayek had in mind. With respect to their welfare, choosers know best, and we respect their liberty for that reason. They do not suffer from "our irremediable ignorance."

There are many good justifications for active choosing, but there is also a tempting justification that falls somewhat short. The claim is that in many contexts people affirmatively like to choose and active choosing is desirable for that reason. The premise is certainly correct. Sometimes people really do prefer to choose, and indeed they may want to retain their authority to choose even if relinquishing it to someone else—say, an expert—would be in their economic interest.[11] (In chapter 5, I focus on the other side of the story.) The idea of "choice bias" refers to the fact that people show a strong preference for options they have actually chosen over equally good options that have not come to them as a result of their own free choice.[12] People

10. *See* Joseph Raz, The Morality of Freedom (1985).
11. *See* Ernst Fehr et al., *The Lure of Authority: Motivation and Incentive Effects of Power*, 103 Am. Econ. Rev. 1325, 1326 (2013).
12. *See* Jeffrey Cockburn, Anne G. E. Collins, & Michael J. Frank, *A Reinforcement Learning Mechanism Responsible for the Valuation of Free Choice*, 83 Neuron 551 (2014).

choose what they prefer, but they also prefer what they choose. If so, they might well also prefer to retain the right to choose. This point argues strongly against coercion in the form of mandates and bans. But it is not an objection to the use of default rules. If such rules are in place, people do retain freedom of choice, and they can reject the default if they want to exercise that freedom.

True, it may be best for choice architects to ask active choosers whether they *want* to rely on a default rather than simply imposing one, but in either case people are free to choose. The strongest arguments on behalf of active choosing lie elsewhere.

OVERCOMING INERTIA

Because a decision is required, active choosing overcomes inertia, as a default rule will not. Suppose that inertia and procrastination are playing a significant role in ensuring that people fail to give serious consideration to the possibility that the current default rule is not in their interest. If so, active choosing may be an excellent corrective, even if it is mandatory. Such choosing requires people to incur "effort costs" that they might otherwise refuse to incur or might expend on other matters.

Consider savings plans, health insurance, and privacy settings. The problem with an opt-in default rule is that it will likely mean that some people will be saddled with outcomes that are quite harmful and that they would not select if they were to make a choice. A key virtue of active choosing is that it increases the likelihood that people will end up with their desired outcomes. For this reason, it might well make sense for choice architects to favor it.

Or return to the case of organ donation. With opt-in, a lot of people stick with the status quo, in part because they do not want to think about a question that is not much fun to ponder. But to some people, the very idea of opt-out is offensive on religious or moral grounds. In Israel, for example, some religious groups have not been enthusiastic about opt-out, which turns people into potential organ donors even though they have not given their explicit consent. The advantage of active choosing is that it avoids the moral objection while also overcoming inertia by getting people to focus on the issue. Outside of the context of organ donation, recall the problem of cognitive scarcity: A virtue of active choosing is that if such scarcity is leading people not to devote attention to an important matter, choice architects can activate attention by asking people to choose. To be sure, prompted choice can have that effect without actually requiring choice—but if the goal is to overcome inertia, required choice might be more effective.[13]

OVERCOMING BAD CHOICE ARCHITECTS

The knowledge problem. In many contexts, choice architects lack relevant information, ensuring that the chosen rule will be harmful to some or many. If so, there are significant advantages to active choosing, and choosers might appreciate that fact. Suppose that a private institution is producing the default rule and really does not know a great deal about what informed people would choose. In the context of ice cream flavors, tablets, cell phones, and sneakers, people tend to know what they like or are willing to learn. While advice might be welcome, active choosing is far better than an impersonal default rule.

---

13. Recall, however, the interesting finding in Kessler & Roth, *supra* note 3, to the effect that prompted choice is more effective than required choice in the context of organ donation.

The same is true for many activities and goods provided by private institutions, including a wide range of businesses that sell goods or services. Market pressures should not be romanticized, especially in view of behavioral biases, but under appropriate conditions those pressures can lead institutions to a good mix of default rules and active choosing, fitting the desires of diverse customers. At a restaurant, you might well ask the waiter to choose for you, and you might even welcome a default menu, but a lot of people prefer to choose for themselves.

Or suppose that the government is producing the default rule. In some cases, public officials might be biased, focusing on their own narrow interests (such as reelection). In other cases, officials might be inadequately informed because the problem is complicated and technical, and because they do not have enough information to solve it. If they select a default rule that is no better than a guess, that rule might lead people in the wrong direction. Dedicated followers of Hayek emphasize what they call "the knowledge problem," which stems from the fact that knowledge is widely dispersed in society, and public officials will not have access to that dispersed knowledge. For Hayek, the price system is far better than the decisions of any group of officials, because it incorporates the dispersed knowledge of the countless people who make purchasing decisions. Consider, by way of analogy, this remarkable passage from Hayek himself:

> This is, perhaps, also the point where I should briefly mention the fact that the sort of knowledge with which I have been concerned is knowledge of the kind which by its nature cannot enter into statistics and therefore cannot be conveyed to any central authority in statistical form. The statistics which such a central authority would have to use would have to be arrived at precisely by abstracting from minor differences between the things, by lumping together, as resources of one kind, items which differ as regards location, quality, and other particulars,

in a way which may be very significant for the specific decision. It follows from this that central planning based on statistical information by its nature cannot take direct account of these circumstances of time and place and that the central planner will have to find some way or other in which the decisions depending on them can be left to the "man on the spot."[14]

Hayek was not speaking of default rules, but in light of this passage, it is possible to fear that public officials will set default rules that are far too crude. If local knowledge is what counts—if what matters is the "man on the spot"—there would seem to be good reason to favor active choosing.

Public choice. The same point argues against a default rule and in favor of active choosing whenever self-interested private groups are calling for government to select a particular rule even though it would not benefit those on whom it is imposed. Here, then, is the "public choice" problem, associated above all with the economist James Buchanan, which refers to the possibility—indeed, the likelihood—that public officials will be influenced by private groups whose interests are entirely selfish. If the public choice problem is serious, default rules will reflect the concerns of self-interested private groups, which seek rules that will benefit them, and not the public as a whole. Perhaps consumers will be defaulted into outcomes that serve the interests of sellers of particular goods and services. In the nightmare scenario—which is far from unrealistic—the knowledge problem and the public choice problem turn out to be mutually reinforcing when public officials, lacking important information, move in directions that reflect the wishes (and knowledge) of those with particular influence over them.

Active choosing is much less risky on these counts. If private citizens should not and do not trust public officials—perhaps

14. Friedrich Hayek, *The Use of Knowledge in Society*, 35 Am. Econ. Rev. 518, 524 (1945).

because they do not know enough, perhaps because their motivations are not pure, or both—they might like active choosing best. The power of interest groups should be underlined. If an interest group can drive a default rule in its preferred direction, it might be best to insist on active choosing instead. Good choice architects might insist on exactly that, and choosers, in the form of citizens and voters, might encourage them to do so.

Choice architecture for choice architects. In the abstract, the underlying considerations are not obscure. But with respect to the trustworthiness of choice architects, there are real complications. Choice architects may not be sufficiently attentive to their own ignorance or biases. Unrealistic optimism, or some kind of self-serving bias, might lead private or public actors to have an inflated sense of their own capacity to design sensible default rules. Public officials are emphatically human and subject to behavioral biases, and the same is true of those who run (for example) corporations and religious organizations.

I have referred to two important safeguards: democratic accountability and market pressures. If governments create terrible default rules—making people's lives poorer, shorter, less convenient, or otherwise worse—they will suffer electoral retribution, at least if democracy is working well and people are paying enough attention. Recall that default rules should be transparent and subject to scrutiny. If so, public officials will be accountable for bad default rules. And if a company defaults people into situations that work out poorly, it will not stay in business very long. Some kind of choice architecture is necessary for choice architects, and democratic safeguards (including a high degree of transparency) are a good way to constrain government, just as well-functioning and free markets will discipline private institutions.

Nonetheless, the knowledge problem and the public choice problem are real even in the most well-functioning democracies.

I have also emphasized that private institutions get away with harmful default rules even if market pressures are robust; behavioral biases are one reason. If people are unrealistically optimistic or if they do not pay attention, they might be victimized by bad defaults. Good regulators can respond to that problem—but that point brings us back to the need to devise institutional safeguards to increase the likelihood that regulators will be good. All of these points argue against default rules and on behalf of active choosing.

HANDLING CHANGES OVER TIME

Default rules tend to be static, and if people's situations change over time, such rules might not be ideal even if they were sensible when originally imposed.[15] A default health plan may make sense for you when you are in your twenties, but when you are in your fifties, it might not suit you at all. With respect to privacy, your preferences might change over time. By contrast, active choosing can be designed in such a way as to require periodic revelation of a chooser's preferences. In markets, a degree of dynamism is essentially guaranteed. People purchase goods and services as they want or need them. As they develop new tastes (for, say, soap, sneakers, or cell phones), those tastes are registered at the time of purchase.

In theory, of course, default rules could also change over time. An all-knowing choice architect could project how tastes are likely to evolve, perhaps by generalizing from the behavior of large populations. Choice architects might know, for example, that young people are more likely to select certain health insurance plans and older

---

15. See James Choi et al., *Defined Contribution Pensions: Plan Rules, Participant Decisions, and the Path of Least Resistance, in* Tax Policy and the Economy (James Poterba ed., 2002).

people are more likely to select very different plans. But in practice, and outside the context of a few relatively clear cases, it might not be so easy to produce accurate projections, at least at the level of individuals.

To be sure, this challenge might be surmounted over time, especially with the rise of large data sets, which are steadily improving our ability to project what informed people are likely to choose. But even so, data-driven default rules might reflect choosers' particular situations less accurately than active choosing would. It is true that choosers themselves might choose to run the risk of inaccuracy and thus choose not to choose, especially if they are not much interested in the area at hand or if the stakes are relatively low. But in many cases, the possibility of changes over time argue strongly in favor of active choosing.

HETEROGENEITY

People are of course differently situated, and in many situations active choosing appropriately handles diversity. As compared with either opt-in or opt-out, active choosing can have major advantages when the relevant group is heterogeneous, so that a single approach will not fit diverse circumstances. If one size does not fit all for health insurance, website settings, or savings, for example, then choice architects might want to ensure that people make choices on their own.

In the face of diversity, a default rule might be especially harmful if the power of inertia, or the force of suggestion, means that many people will end up in a situation that is not in their interest. When people's situations differ, they might be far better off if they are asked "what health insurance plan do you like best?" than if they are automatically enrolled in a plan their employer has chosen.

It is true that freedom of choice, in the form of the ability to opt out, is an important safeguard against the problem of one-size-fits-all approaches. But because of the effects of inertia and the power of suggestion, some people will stick with a default even when it really does not fit their situation. And it is true that a personalized default rule, designed to fit people's diverse situations, might reduce the problem of heterogeneity. I will discuss that possibility in due course. But the design of personalized defaults can present serious challenges of its own, especially when the choice architects have limited information. If the relevant group is diverse, there is a strong argument for active choosing, because it promotes accuracy.

LEARNING, AGENCY, AND DIGNITY

The last points may be the most important. By definition, active choosing is a reflection of individual agency. It also promotes learning and thus the development of preferences, values, and tastes. John Stuart Mill made the essential point, emphasizing that "the free development of individuality is one of the leading essentials of well-being" and indeed that "it is not only a coordinate element with all that is designated by the terms civilization, instruction, education, culture, but is itself a necessary part and condition of all those things."[16] Mill noted that conformity to custom "does not educate or develop...any of the qualities which are the distinctive endowment of a human being. The human faculties of perception, judgment, discriminative feeling, mental activity, are exercised only in making a choice. He who does anything because it is the custom, makes no choice. He gains no practice either in discerning or in desiring what is best. The mental and moral, like the muscular

---

16. JOHN STUART MILL, ON LIBERTY 102 (2d ed., 1869) (1859).

powers, are improved only by being used."[17] A default rule might well be seen as a reflection of custom, which is Mill's particular concern. Individual dignity is at stake as well. If the goal is to cultivate a sense of self-respect, active choosing would seem to have significant advantages over a system in which people merely follow, or do not disturb, rules laid down by others.

The basic problem. With respect to learning, there is strong evidence that Mill was right. Consider the GPS, which creates a kind of default route, on which people can rely, but which they can reject if they see fit. Almost no one would prefer a world without the GPS, but it does have a serious downside, which is that use of the GPS can make it harder for people to learn how to navigate the roads on their own. Indeed, London taxi drivers, not relying on the GPS, have been found to experience an alteration of their neurological functioning as they learn more about navigation, with actual changes in physical regions of the brain.[18] With the widespread use of the GPS, that kind of alteration will not occur, thus ensuring that people cannot navigate without some mechanical help. The default rule makes life easier to navigate, but it impedes learning.

This is an unusually dramatic finding, to be sure, but it should be taken as a metaphor for a wide range of actual and potential effects of defaults. It raises the possibility that when people rely on defaults rather than their own active choices, some important human capacities will fail to develop or may atrophy. This is an unfortunate consequence of sensible default rules: They prevent people from learning and developing their capacities. If the brain is seen as a muscle, it can become weak or strong, and choice-making is a kind of exercise that may strengthen it.

17. *Id.*
18. Eleanor A. Maguire et al., *Navigation-Related Structural Changes in the Hippocampi of Taxi Drivers*, 97 PROC. NAT'L ACAD. SCI. 4398 (2000).

We can easily imagine a kind of science-fiction tale, depicting a Brave New World in which people are defaulted into a large number of good outcomes, or even choose to be so defaulted, but are deprived of agency and in an important sense dignity. In the words of Aldous Huxley's foreword to his great novel: "A really efficient totalitarian state would be one in which the all-powerful executive of political bosses and their army of managers control a population of slaves who do not have to be coerced, because they love their servitude."[19] George Orwell's *1984* points to a system without liberty, but in Huxley's book, the assault on dignity is at least as sinister, because the pursuit of comfort and pleasure erodes agency. Many people fear that default rules threaten to infantilize people, and their underlying concern lies here. Consider the second epigraph for this book— the pleas of Huxley's hero, the Savage, surrounded by a world of comfortable defaults:

"But I don't want comfort. I want God, I want poetry, I want real danger, I want freedom, I want goodness. I want sin."

"In fact," said Mustapha Mond, "you're claiming the right to be unhappy."

"All right then," said the Savage defiantly, "I'm claiming the right to be unhappy."

"Not to mention the right to grow old and ugly and impotent; the right to have syphilis and cancer; the right to have too little to eat, the right to be lousy; the right to live in constant apprehension of what may happen tomorrow; the right to catch typhoid; the right to be tortured by unspeakable pains of every kind."

There was a long silence.

"I claim them all," said the Savage at last.[20]

---

19. ALDOUS HUXLEY, BRAVE NEW WORLD xii (1931).
20. *Id.* at 163.

Such objections should not be romanticized (as Huxley tended to do) or overstated. Syphilis and cancer, typhoid and torture, and having too little to eat are likely to be "claimed" only by those who have never suffered from those things. And there are some capacities that it is not so important to cultivate. Human beings have lost the capacity to memorize pages and pages of text; is that a serious loss? Egypt's King Thamus lamented that if people depended on writing, the result would be to "weaken men's characters and create forgetfulness in their souls."[21] But it is hard to say that people would be better off if they had to rely on memorization. Nonetheless, there are important domains in which learning is important and active choosing is necessary to promote it.

Choosers may themselves favor active choosing and reject defaults because they want to develop their own faculties and exercise their own agency. Choice architects, for their part, might know that a certain outcome is in the interest of most people but might also believe that it is important for people to learn about the underlying questions so that they can develop a kind of capital stock and use that stock to make good choices in the future. In the context of financial decisions, it might be valuable for people to develop the kinds of understandings that will enable them to choose well for themselves. The "stock" might turn out to be helpful for the remainder of their lives. More generally, exercise of the choice-making muscle might have desirable spillover effects in other areas of life, developing an active rather than passive approach to a wide range of decisions. A world of default rules, making passivity both easy and pervasive, could have serious negative spillovers, producing an inert and torpid citizenry, hopelessly dependent on those rules.

21. Daniel Levitin, The Organized Mind 14 (2014).

The same point holds for decisions relating to health care. With respect to health insurance, choosers may wish to choose, not because they enjoy the process but because they believe that what they learn will help them over the long term. Perhaps choice architects agree. Or consider the practice of medicine. Some doctors might be tempted to choose some kind of default rule in difficult cases and to suggest that patients ought to rely on it. But other doctors might reject that approach in favor of a strong presumption of patient autonomy, offering information but asking for an active choice, in part so that patients learn.

The point is not to suggest any particular judgment about these examples. (In the medical context, my own view is that doctors should be relying far more on default rules, at least in the form of recommendations based on the best available evidence. One reason is that many patients choose not to choose, and it is both an intrusion and potentially even a form of cruelty to override their choice—a point to which I will return.) It might well turn out that in any specific context, the justification for active choosing is unconvincing. But there are certainly domains in which learning is important and active choosing is necessary to promote it. Here, then, is an enduring argument for active choosing.

There are related points about responsibility and authenticity. If you have made your own choice about end-of-life care or about healthy eating, you have exercised responsibility for your own well-being. It is fair to say that the relevant choices are authentically yours. If the outcomes have come by default, the same cannot be said. If responsibility and authenticity are important, either in themselves or for instrumental reasons, then active choosing has major advantages over default rules.

An objection to automaticity. These points raise concerns about any approach that defaults people into specific outcomes solely on the basis of their own past choices. Suppose, for example, that a political system defaulted people into voting for political candidates of the same party for which they previously voted (subject to opt-out). Such a system would unquestionably reduce the burdens of voting, simply because people's preferences would be registered automatically. For many voters, that system would be desirable, because it would make life a lot more convenient—reducing the costs of decisions without much increasing the costs of errors. But there is a strong argument that it would be inconsistent with a defining goal of a democratic system, which is to ensure continual learning and scrutiny by voters, not simply a single decision in an initial period. Even if default rules reduced burdens—as they undoubtedly would—part of the point of a democratic system is to impose those burdens, or even to consider them privileges, so as to ensure that self-government is real.

If that goal is taken seriously, there is reason to object not only to "default voting" based on people's past choices but also to a system in which people actively choose to enroll in default voting, on the ground that the aspiration to learning and continuing scrutiny forbids even active enrollment into default voting. If people could enroll into default voting, the registration of preferences and values would, in a sense, be too automatic, because it would not reflect any kind of active, current judgment about candidates and issues.

As a preliminary test of how people think about that issue, I conducted a small experiment at Harvard University, asking about seventy students the following question:

> You live in a state that is considering a system of "default voting," in accordance with which people could set up party-line votes in advance. In this system, they could go online, at any time, to partyvote.gov, and say that they want to vote for all

Republicans or all Democrats in the coming election. What do you think of this idea? (Assume the site is completely secure.)

A strong majority (79 percent) disapproved of the idea. Interestingly, over one-fifth approved of it, apparently on the ground that it would increase convenience. But the widespread disapproval testifies to a norm in favor of a more active form of participation.

I also asked a different group of people, recruited from Amazon Mechanical Turk, the same question, and here the numbers were essentially identical, with 78 percent (of a total of fifty) rejecting that system. It is possible that such disapproval merely reflects a contemporary social norm, which could be changed as technology evolves. Perhaps default voting will have more appeal in the future. But the current norm might well be taken to suggest a wholly defensible social judgment in favor of relatively active, and continuing, engagement in the process of choosing among candidates.

Or consider the website Pandora, which allows people to identify a favorite song or singer and devises a kind of default music "station" on the basis of that choice. The website has many virtues, and it is a ton of fun. If you say that you like Bob Dylan, Aimee Mann, or the Dave Matthews Band or that your favorite song is Taylor Swift's "Mean," you'll get a large number of selections that you like, and you'll love some of them, and you'll also be surprised by what you hear. The selections can be understood as (personalized) defaults, based on what you say you like. But there is a risk to learning and self-development in any situation in which people are defaulted into a kind of echo chamber, even if they themselves took the initial step to devise it.[22] Maybe people should broaden their horizons, and if their stations consist only of Bob Dylan Radio, Aimee Mann

22. For an extended argument to this effect, see CASS R. SUNSTEIN, REPUBLIC.COM (2001).

Radio, Dave Matthews Band Radio, and Mean Radio, they will be a bit self-insulating.

The same might be said about Netflix, which does not exactly use defaults (in the sense of playing music or movies even when one does nothing) but which does assemble a set of suggestions based on people's previous choices and evaluations.[23] Netflix's distinctive kind of fine-tuning, which produces a great deal of precision in the resulting suggestions, obviously brings about large welfare benefits, because people see what they are highly likely to like (and they can choose it—actively, not by default). The question is whether the welfare benefits come at a cost, in the form of inevitable self-narrowing, simply because the relevant suggestions are based on previous choices and do not encourage people to branch out.

A great city combats such narrowing, because of the dazzling range of serendipitous encounters it promotes.[24] In a sense, it allows people to choose not to choose—and what they do not choose surprises and enriches them. There is a large difference between an *architecture of control*, based on past choices, and an *architecture of serendipity*, in which one stumbles on new topics, perspectives, and things. It could well be argued that an architecture of serendipity is more compatible with self-development and (along an important dimension) with liberty itself. (It is ironic that the app StumbleUpon creates personalized profiles and communities of like-minded people; it ensures that you "stumble upon" things that fit with your tastes and past choices.) I return to these concerns in part III.

A counter-argument. Let us step back from the particular examples and notice that there is a serious objection to an argument for

---

23. Cosimo Birtolo et al., *Personalized Suggestions by Means of Collaborative Filtering: A Comparison of Two Different Model-Based Techniques*, Nature and Biologically Inspired Computing (NaBIC), 2011 Third World Congress on IEEE, 2011.
24. *See* Jane Jacobs, The Death and Life of Great American Cities (1961).

active choosing that is based on learning and associated values. The objection is that *people do and should learn about whether to choose actively—or instead to choose not to choose.*[25] People sometimes decide correctly and sometimes err in making that particular choice, as in making all other choices. It is important for people to learn, over time, about when they should be choosing and when they should be relying on a default rule (and accepting the force of inertia or the power of suggestion).[26] That form of second-order learning is exceedingly important.

In this light, the problem is that those who insist on active choosing, or even merely favor or promote it, will reduce or prevent learning along this important dimension. Claiming to cherish learning and the development of values and preferences, they truncate such learning and such development about an extremely important question: *whether to choose actively.*

In light of this objection, the argument from learning must be more refined. It must be that in particular cases, it is especially important that people engage in first-order rather than second-order learning, because the subject is one for which they should accumulate some kind of "capital"—as, for example, by learning about what they actually like (in terms of, say, politics, art, or music) or by developing an understanding of certain matters that very much affect how their lives will unfold over time (in terms of, say, health insurance or investments).

In some such cases, the argument for active choosing, based on this more refined argument, is convincing. But there is another side to this particular coin; let's turn to it.

---

25. I am grateful to Adrian Vermeule for pressing this point.
26. *See* N. Craig Smith et al., *Choice Without Awareness*, 32 J. Pub. Pol'y & Marketing 159, 161 (2013).

[5]

CHOICE-REQUIRING
PATERNALISM

A lot of people believe that there is a clear opposition between paternalism and active choosing. In many cases, however, that opposition is an illusion. An insistence on active choosing is often a form of paternalism, not an alternative to it.

We have identified the principal reason that this is so: some people choose not to choose. Sometimes they make that choice explicitly (and indeed may be willing to pay a considerable amount to people who will choose for them). Sometimes people have made no explicit choice; they have not actively chosen anything. But it is nonetheless reasonable to infer that in particular contexts, their preference is not to choose, and they would say so if they were asked. Recall the diversity of reasons: They might fear that they will err. They might be aware of their own lack of information or perhaps their own behavioral biases (such as present bias or unrealistic optimism).[1] They might find the underlying questions confusing, difficult, painful, and troublesome—empirically, morally, or otherwise. They might not enjoy choosing. They might be busy and lack "bandwidth." They might anticipate their own regret and seek to

---

1. On the effects of lack of information in producing abstention, see Tom Coupe & Abdul Noury, *Choosing Not to Choose: On the Link Between Information and Abstention*, 84 ECON. LETTERS 261 (2004).

avoid it. They might not want to take responsibility for potentially bad outcomes for themselves (and at least indirectly for others).[2]

An important clarification: It is necessary to distinguish between (1) an active choice to choose someone else to choose for you and (2) not choosing, which involves making no choice at all. You might choose not to choose—in the sense of (1)—for the various reasons just listed. By contrast, you might not choose in the sense of (2) because (for example) of procrastination or because you want to retain your options. Sometimes choosing feels like losing, and people do not like to lose.[3] There is of course an overlap between choosing not to choose and not choosing. People might decline to choose because they are busy, do not want to take responsibility, or think that they might err. But choosing not to choose, which is my principal topic here, is very different from not choosing at all.

Even when people prefer not to choose, many private and public institutions favor and promote active choosing on the ground that it is good for people to choose. To this extent, active choosing counts as paternalistic. To be sure, "nanny states" forbid choosing, but they also forbid the choice not to choose. *Choice-requiring paternalism* is sometimes an attractive form of paternalism, but it is no oxymoron, and it is paternalistic nonetheless.

If people are *required* to choose when they would prefer not to do so, active choosing counts as a species of nonlibertarian paternalism in the sense that people's own choices are being rejected. In many cases, those who favor active choosing are actually mandating it and may therefore be overriding, on paternalistic grounds, people's choice not to choose. (There is an irony here in light of

2. For a demonstration, see Björn Bartling & Urs Fischbacher, *Shifting the Blame: On Delegation and Responsibility*, 79 REV. ECON. STUD. 67 (2012).
3. *See* Ziv Carmon et al., *Option Attachment: When Deliberating Makes Choosing Feel Like Losing*, 30 J. CONST. RES. 15 (2003).

evidence that people sometimes place an excessive value on choice, in the sense that their preference for choice leads them to suffer welfare losses, as they devote time and effort to making selections that are not particularly good.)[4] When people prefer not to choose, required choosing is a form of coercion—though it may be the right form, at least where active choosing does not increase the likelihood and magnitude of errors and where it is important to enable people to learn, to express their own agency, and to develop their own preferences.

If, by contrast, people are *asked whether they want to choose* and can opt out of active choosing (in favor of, say, a default rule), then active choosing counts as a form of libertarian paternalism. In some cases, it is an especially attractive form. Call it *simplified active choosing.* A company might ask people whether they want to choose the privacy settings on their computer or rely on the default, or whether they want to choose their electricity supplier or instead rely on the default. With simplified active choosing, people are being asked to make an active choice between the default and their own preference, and in that sense their liberty is fully preserved. This approach has the advantage of reducing the kinds of influences that come from a default rule while also allowing people to rely on such a rule if they like. I have already mentioned a variation on this approach: prompted choosing, by which people are asked whether they want to choose ("do you want to be an organ donor?") but are free to ignore the question, in which case some kind of default rule applies.

It is important to see, however, that whenever a private or public institution asks people to choose, it might be overriding their preference not to do so and in that sense engaging in choice-requiring

---

4. *See* Simona Botti & Christopher Hsee, *Dazed and Confused by Choice*, 112 ORG. BEHAV. AND HUM. DECISION PROCESSES 161 (2010).

paternalism. This point applies *even when people are being asked whether they want to choose to choose*. After all, they might not want to make that second-order choice (and might therefore prefer a simple default rule). They might find the request tiring, irritating, intrusive, or annoying. (A spouse, a romantic partner, or a friend who constantly asks you whether you want to choose might seem kind and generous but might become really irritating.) In this sense, there is a strong nonlibertarian dimension to apparently liberty-preserving approaches that ask people to choose between active choosing and a default rule. If these claims do not seem self-evident, or if they appear a bit jarring, it is because the idea of active choosing is so familiar in well-functioning democracies and so obviously appealing that it may not be seen for what it is: a form of choice architecture, and one that many choosers may dislike, at least in settings that are unfamiliar or difficult.[5]

Building on the discussion in chapter 4, I aim to show here that whether people should favor active choosing or should instead choose not to choose depends on a set of identifiable questions, generally (but not only) involving the costs of decisions and the costs of errors. The idea of minimizing the sum of decision costs and error costs may well be the most important general contribution of the economic analysis of law, because it helps to untie many conceptual knots. It is a simple and intuitive way of engaging in cost-benefit analysis. If people have to spend considerable time and energy to make decisions, they incur significant costs—but if they enjoy expending that time and energy, they are obtaining benefits. If people's own choices would lead in directions that would make their lives go exceptionally well, and if default rules would produce numerous and large mistakes, then there are no error costs from

---

5. A valuable discussion is presented in Barbara Fried, *But Seriously, Folks, What Do People Want?*, 65 Stan. L. Rev. 1529 (2013).

active choosing, which is (on those assumptions) likely to produce significant benefits as compared with default rules.

Suppose that private or public institutions lack relevant knowledge, are self-interested, or are subject to the pressures imposed by selfish private groups. If so, there is a strong argument for active choosing, because that approach will reduce the costs of errors. And if choosing is a benefit rather than a cost because people like it, there is a further reason for active choosing. In such cases, people should choose to choose. But if the area is complex, technical, difficult, novel, and not a lot of fun, there is a strong argument against active choosing, because it will increase decision costs and potentially error costs as well. Another question is whether people believe that choosing is intrinsically desirable or not, perhaps because it is a way of exercising their freedom and authority.[6] Often they do, but choosing not to choose is itself a form of choice and may be an active one (and may be intrinsically desirable). A pervasive question is whether it is important for people to exercise their own agency (and perhaps to learn from the exercise).

There is undoubtedly a great deal of diversity here, across both people and contexts.[7] Some people generally choose not to choose; others abhor that approach. (A moment's introspection can often reveal what kind of tendency you have.) An area that is technical for some people might be child's play for others. We know that choice can be a lot of fun or a big bother; of course the context matters.

6. For strong evidence that people do believe that choosing is intrinsically valuable, see Björn Bartling et al., *The Intrinsic Value of Decision Rights* (U. of Zurich, Dep't of Econ. Working Paper No. 120, 2013), *available at* http://papers.ssrn.com/sol3/papers.cfm?abstract_id=2255992. *See also* Ricardo Rebonato, *A Critical Assessment of Libertarian Paternalism*, 37 J. CONSUMER POL'Y 357, 382 (2014) ("Failing to make (or rarely making) this important distinction between the outcome in itself and the full choice process (outcome plus the ability or otherwise of choosing) is at the root of the widespread absence in the libertarian paternalistic literature of a sympathetic treatment of autonomy.").

7. For a finding of a general commitment to the intrinsic value of the power to decide, cutting across a relatively diverse population, see Bartling et al., *supra* note 6.

Some people like to choose among dresses while other people abhor that particular task. For some people, it's kind of fun to go shopping for a new pair of shoes; for others it's a form of torture. Some people in some contexts would be willing to pay a premium to have the power to choose themselves, other things being equal.[8]

Compare the related phenomenon of "reactance," which refers to people's negative reaction to efforts to control or restrict them, produced in part by their desire to assert their autonomy. Jack Brehm has explored that phenomenon in detail, showing its preconditions and establishing that when people think that someone is taking away their options or attempting to control them, they may react negatively in a way that increases their resistance.[9] The result may well be a strengthened commitment to their original belief, desire, or plan of action. When choice architects encourage people not to choose, or even establish defaults, the risk of reactance cannot be ruled out.

But some people in some contexts are willing to pay a premium to have someone else choose for them, other things being equal. They are eager to have or even to hire an agent. Sometimes people do not show reactance at all. Indeed, they tend to show the opposite, a kind of heightened receptivity—call it *receptance*—as they welcome architectures or initiatives that make choices easier or unnecessary or allow passive choosing. People tend to have an intuitive appreciation of these points and to incorporate them into their judgments about whether and when to choose. In well-functioning families, a principle of considerateness tends to ensure that people

---

8. Ernst Fehr et al., *The Lure of Authority: Motivation and Incentive Effects of Power*, 103 Am. Econ. Rev. 1325 (2013).

9. *See* Sharon Brehm & Jack Brehm, Psychological Reactance: A Theory of Freedom and Control (1981); Louisa Pavey & Paul Sparks, *Reactance, Autonomy and Paths to Persuasion: Examining Perceptions of Threats to Freedom and Informational Value*, 33 Motivation & Emotion 277 (2009).

allocate responsibilities in a way that reflects when people like to choose and when they do not.[10]

An investigation of particular areas often reveals both the force and the weakness of the argument for active choosing. Many restaurants do best with a large menu offering people diverse items, but tourists in unfamiliar nations may well prefer a default menu—a difference that reflects the costs of decisions and the costs of errors. An interesting question is whether, in identifiable contexts, people are too willing to choose (for example, because of overconfidence) or insufficiently willing (for example, because of excessive trust in certain institutions). There is little doubt that both mistakes occur.

At first glance, it would seem that the choice between active choosing and some kind of default rule, based in part on decision costs and error costs, should be made by choosers themselves, at least if the interests of third parties are not involved. If choosers choose not to choose or if that is what they would choose if asked, their choice should generally be respected. To that extent, choice-requiring paternalism should usually be avoided. Unless some kind of market failure is involved, including a behavioral market failure (such as present bias), private and public institutions should not insist on active choosing when people prefer not to choose—just as they should not insist on a default rule when people prefer active choosing.

Of course, the "unless" clause is important; people's decision not to choose might not serve their interests. If so, some kind of intervention might be desirable, perhaps in the form of a nudge (such as disclosure of relevant information or a warning). We have seen an additional qualification: the argument for active choosing gains strength when learning, authenticity, responsibility, and the

---

10. *See* Edna Ullmann-Margalit, *Family Fairness*, 73 Soc. Res. 575 (2006).

development of values and preferences are important. In such cases, choice-requiring paternalism has a lot of appeal. This point raises a significant cautionary note about any program that defaults people into goods or services on the basis of their own previous choices—a seemingly attractive approach that might nonetheless prove an obstacle to learning by people in their roles as both consumers and citizens. In such cases, choice-requiring paternalism is no oxymoron, and it has strong justifications. Some evidence, which I present in part III, suggests that people have an intuitive appreciation of this point as well.

VARIETIES OF CHOICE

Many of those who embrace active choosing believe that consumers of goods and services should be free from government influence. Of course they recognize that in markets, producers will impose influences of multiple kinds, but they contend that when third parties are not affected and force and fraud are not involved, government should remain neutral. They reject paternalism on government's part. Perhaps it is legitimate for public officials to require the provision of accurate information, so as to ensure that consumer's choices are adequately informed. But if government seeks to default people in its preferred directions in other ways—by embracing paternalism of any kind—it is exceeding its appropriate bounds. On this view, people cannot be made free by default.

But what does active choosing entail?[11] Consider three possibilities. For shorthand, we can refer to them as direct penalties,

11. I am understanding the term in a purely formal sense, to capture a response to a question about what one prefers. It would be possible to understand "choosing" in a more functional sense, to capture deciding for reasons, as distinguished from simply "picking," which is akin to tossing a coin. For an important discussion, see Edna Ullmann-Margalit & Sidney Morgenbesser, *Picking and Choosing*, 44 Soc. Res. 757

leveraging, and ordinary market arrangements; each raises its own complexities.

Direct penalties. In most contexts, no one contends that if people fail to make a choice they should be imprisoned or otherwise punished. The sanction for that failure is that they do not receive a good or service. But there are exceptions. In some nations, including Australia, Belgium, and (before 1970) the Netherlands, people have been subject to civil sanctions if they fail to vote and in that sense could be punished for refusing to make an active choice.[12] So, too, the Affordable Care Act requires people to make a choice about health insurance, subject to a tax penalty if they fail to do so.

With respect to active choosing, both of these cases do have a wrinkle: People are being forced to choose along one dimension (for whom to vote and which health insurance plan to obtain) but are being prohibited from choosing along another dimension (whether to vote or to obtain health insurance). But insofar as one kind of choice is being required, it is fair to speak of required active choosing. We could imagine other contexts in which people would face sanctions if they do not choose, though admittedly such cases look more like science fiction than the real world. Consider cases in which people must decide whether to become organ donors (or face criminal penalties) or must choose privacy settings on their computer (subject to civil sanctions if they do not).

The fact that sanctions are rarely imposed on people who choose not to choose should be taken to suggest an implicit recognition that in a free society, such choices are generally acceptable and indeed a legitimate part of liberty. We have seen that one reason involves information. People know best what they want, and others should

(1977). As I understand it here, active choosing includes "picking," and can occur even when people lack an antecedent preference.

12. Lisa Hill, *Low Voter Turnout in the United States: Is Compulsory Voting a Solution*, 18 J. THEORETICAL POL. 207, 208 (2006).

not choose for them, even if the choice is not to choose. There is some good and somewhat amusing empirical support for this view: During holiday season, even family members and close friends often choose gifts that people do not much like—resulting in billions of dollars in annual losses (reflecting the fact that the gifts are worth less to the recipients than they cost).[13] If family members and close friends make mistakes, can government possibly avoid them?

Leveraging. Sometimes active choosing is mandatory in a distinctive sense: Unless people make an active choice on some matter, they cannot obtain a good or service, even though that good or service, narrowly defined, is not the specific topic of the choice that they are being asked to make. In this sense, a form of leveraging is involved. It is possible to imagine a continuum of connections between the matter in question, for which an active choice is being required, and the specific good that has already been chosen. There would be a close connection if, for example, people were told that unless they indicated their preferences with respect to motor vehicle insurance, they could not rent motor vehicles. So, too, there would be a close connection if people were told that unless they created a password, or indicated their preferences with respect to privacy settings, they could not use their computers. Indeed, both of these cases are standard. In markets, sellers sometimes insist that purchasers must make an active choice on some related matter in order to obtain or use a product.

By contrast, there would be a somewhat weaker connection if people were informed that they could not work with a particular employer until they indicated their preferences with respect

---

13. *See* Joel Waldfogel, Scroogenomics: Why You Shouldn't Buy Presents for the Holidays (2009) (showing that even family members and close friends make large mistakes in choosing for people during holiday season).

to their retirement plan. The connection would be weaker still if people were told that they could not obtain a driver's license unless they indicated their preferences with respect to organ donation. The connection would be even weaker if people were told that they could not register to vote unless they made a choice about their preferred privacy settings on their computer.

In the final two examples, there is not a tight connection between the matter on which people are being asked to make a choice and the good that they are specifically seeking.[14] Note that in some cases that fall in this category, the requirement of active choosing has a strongly coercive dimension insofar as the good in question is one that people cannot easily reject (such as a driver's license, a job, or a right to vote).

To make an evaluation of this form of leveraging, it might be important to distinguish between public and private institutions. Perhaps private institutions, disciplined as they are by market forces, should freely compete along this dimension as along others. If people really dislike active choosing, private institutions that require it will be punished, as long as other institutions do not require it and customers prefer them for that reason. Perhaps public institutions should hesitate before requiring people to choose, unless there is a close connection between the good or service in question and the object of active choice. On the other hand, public institutions are disciplined by public accountability, at least in democratic societies. If a public institution is requiring people to choose in order to save lives, and if its strategy is effective, people should hesitate before concluding that it has acted illegitimately.

---

14. There is a counter-argument in the case of organ donations. In 2007, for example, motorcycle accidents accounted for about 20 percent of all organ donations. *See* Stacy Dickert-Conlin et al., *Donorcycles: Motorcycle Helmet Laws and the Supply of Organ Donors*, 54 J.L. & ECON. 907, 912 (2011).

Ordinary market arrangements. In most markets, active choosing among goods, services, or jobs is a condition for obtaining a good, a service, or a job. For consumption decisions in ordinary markets, people are given a range of options and can choose one or more of them or none at all. Unless they make a choice, they will not obtain the relevant good or service. They are not defaulted into purchasing tablets, cell phones, shoes, or fishing poles. When people visit a website, a restaurant, or a grocery or appliance store, they are generally asked to make an active choice. The default—understood as what happens if they do nothing—is that no product will be purchased. People do not receive goods or services unless they have actively chosen them. The same point holds for the employment market. People are not typically defaulted into particular jobs, at least not in any formal sense. They have a range of options, and unless they take one they will be unemployed. In this respect, free markets generally require active choosing. (Of course there are cultural differences on this count, and some less formal kinds of defaults are in place for various practices, emphatically including employment, where young people are effectively defaulted into certain jobs.)

It is important to see that there is nothing inevitable about this situation. It is possible to imagine a situation in which sellers assume, or presume, that people want certain products and buyers obtain them, and have to pay for them, passively. Imagine, for example, that retailers have sufficient information to know for a fact that Johnson would want to buy any new book by Stephen King, Sendhil Mullainathan, or Joyce Carol Oates, that Smith would like to purchase a new version of a particular tablet, that Jones would want to buy a certain pair of sneakers, or that when Williams runs out of toothpaste she would like new toothpaste of exactly the same kind. If the sellers' judgments are unerring, or even nearly so, would it be troublesome and intrusive or instead a great benefit for them to arrange for the relevant purchases by default? Existing technology is increasingly raising this question.

There is a good argument that one of the strongest reasons to require active choosing is that reliable predictive shopping algorithms do not exist. For that reason, active choosing is an indispensable safeguard against erroneous purchases and thus is in the interests of those who might be denominated purchasers (by default). On this view, the argument for active choosing is that affirmative consent protects against mistakes—which leaves open the possibility of predictive shopping if and when a reliable technology becomes available. To the extent that such technology does not exist, predictive shopping would be unacceptable. I return to these issues in part III.

It is true that markets generally require active choosing, but there is a major qualification, which stems from the fact that markets cannot exist without a background set of entitlements. The background entitlements establish what people have and do not have before they begin to choose. Those background entitlements are given rather than chosen. Property rights grant people certain rights and not others, and they provide the foundation for bargaining. True, people might have some kind of "default entitlement" to be free from age discrimination, which they can waive for a price, but some entitlements of this kind (such as the right to be free from discrimination on the basis of race and sex) are not waivable at all.

The important point is that people's preferences may well be affected by official decisions about background entitlements. The most important finding here is the endowment effect: *People tend to value a good more if it is initially allocated to them than if they have to buy it.*[15] Suppose that you are given a lottery ticket or a mug

15. *See* Keith M. Marzilla Ericson & Andreas Fuster, *The Endowment Effect* (Nat'l Bureau of Econ. Research, Working Paper No. 19384, 2013), *available at* www.nber.org/papers/w19384.

with the logo of your favorite sports team. How much would you demand to give it up? The answer is highly likely to be a lot higher than the amount you would be willing to pay to get it in the first place. Recall the vacation study discussed in chapter 1, finding that people would pay only $6,000 to buy two weeks of vacation time but would demand $13,000 to give up those same two weeks. In the area of contracting, it can matter a lot whether people are initially given a right or instead have to buy it.[16]

The lesson is that because of the endowment effect, influences on people's preferences and values may be difficult or perhaps impossible to avoid insofar as some person or institution is making decisions about who gets rights in the first place.[17] If people's preferences are an artifact of entitlements, entitlements cannot be selected by asking what those preferences are.

SELLERS AS CHOICE ARCHITECTS

Sellers often develop a form of choice architecture that features active choosing. But it should be clear that even in domains where it is taken for granted, active choosing is far from inevitable. Instead of opting for active choosing, an institution might select some kind of default rule, specifying what happens if people do nothing.

We have seen that those who obtain driver's licenses might be defaulted into being organ donors, or those who start work with a particular employer might be defaulted into a specific retirement or health care plan. Alternatively, those who make an active choice

---

16. *See* Isabel Marcin & Andreas Nicklisch, *Testing the Endowment Effect for Default Rules* (2014), *available at* http://papers.ssrn.com/sol3/papers.cfm?abstract_id=2375107.
17. I am bracketing the possibility that entitlements are a product of a "spontaneous order" of some sort, rather than of any kind of decision.

to purchase a particular product—say, a book or a subscription to a magazine—might be automatically enrolled into a program to continue to receive a similar product on a periodic basis whether or not they have made an active choice to do so. The old Book of the Month Club famously employed a strategy of this sort.[18]

Strange as it might seem, an active choice to purchase a product might also trigger a default rule that is unrelated to the product— for example, purchase of a particular book might create default enrollment in a health care plan, or an active choice to enroll in a health care plan might create default enrollment in a book club. In extreme cases, where disclosure is insufficiently clear, an approach of this kind might be a form of fraud, though we could imagine cases in which such an approach would merely track people's preferences. Suppose, for example, that a private institution knows that people who purchase products X (say, certain kinds of music) also tend to like products Y (say, certain kinds of books). At least in principle, suggestions of various kinds, default advertisements, default presentations of political views, and perhaps even default purchases could be welcome and in people's interests. For example, the website Pandora tracks people's music preferences, from which it can make some inferences about their likely tastes and judgments about other matters, including politics.[19]

---

18. See Peter Bowal, *Reluctance to Regulate: The Case of Negative Option Marketing*, 36 AM. BUS. L.J. 377, 378–79 (1999).

19. For evidence to this effect, see Natasha Singer, *Listen to Pandora, and It Listens Back*, N.Y. TIMES, Jan. 5, 2014, at BU3, *available at* http://www.nytimes.com/ 2014/01/05/technology/pandora-mines-users-data-to-better-target-ads.html? hpw&rref=technology&_r=2&, and consider in particular: "During the next federal election cycle, for instance, Pandora users tuning into country music acts, stand-up comedians, or Christian bands might hear or see ads for Republican candidates for Congress. Others listening to hip-hop tunes, or to classical acts like the Berlin Philharmonic, might hear ads for Democrats." *Id.*

As a less controversial practice, recall the idea of simplified active choosing, which arises when people are explicitly asked to choose whether they want to choose.[20] Consumers might be asked: Do you want to choose your cell phone settings, or do you want to be defaulted into settings that seem to work best for most people, or for people like you? Do you want to choose your own health insurance plan, or do you want to be defaulted into the plan that seems best for people in your demographic category? With simplified active choosing, many people may well decide in favor of a default rule and thus decline to choose, because of a second-order desire not to do so. They might not trust their own judgment; they might not want to learn. The topic might make them anxious. They might have better things to do.

I have suggested that simplified active choosing has considerable promise and appeal, not least because it avoids many of the influences contained in a default rule and might therefore seem highly respectful of autonomy while also giving people the ability to select the default. For cell phone settings or health insurance plans, choosers can choose actively if they like, while others can (actively) choose the default.

Recall, however, that simplified active choosing is not quite a perfect solution, at least for those people who genuinely do not want to choose. After all, they are being asked to do exactly that. At least some of those people do not want to have to choose between active choosing and a default rule; they would prefer a default rule to an active choice between active choosing and a default rule. Even that active choice takes time and effort and imposes costs, and some or

---

20. *See* Bartling et al., *supra* note 6, which shows that people will often say yes, other things being equal, thus supporting the conclusion that decision rights have intrinsic value. We can agree with that conclusion while also asserting that in some cases, the intrinsic value will be outweighed by the instrumental value of delegation (as, for example, where people believe they will err, or where people are busy).

many people might not want to bother. Notwithstanding its appeal, simplified active choosing itself may be an unwelcome and annoying burden in some contexts.

DOES THE "NANNY STATE" FORBID CHOOSING NOT TO CHOOSE?

Is active choosing paternalistic, when people would prefer not to choose? To answer that question, we have to start by defining paternalism. There is of course an immensely large literature on that topic.[21] Bracketing the hardest issues and noting that diverse definitions have been given, it seems clear that the unifying theme of paternalistic approaches is that *a private or public institution does not believe that people's choices will promote their welfare and is taking steps to influence or alter people's choices for what it considers to be their own good.*[22]

What is wrong with paternalism, thus defined? Those who reject paternalism typically invoke welfare, autonomy, or both.[23] With respect to welfare, they tend to believe that individuals are the best judges of what is in their interests and of what will promote their welfare and that because outsiders lack crucial information, they should not be allowed to intervene. We have seen that John Stuart Mill himself emphasized that this is the essential problem with outsiders, including government officials. Mill's goal was to increase the likelihood that people's lives would go well, and he contended

---

21. *See, e.g.,* PATERNALISM (Christian Coons & Michael Weber eds., 2013); GERALD DWORKIN, THE THEORY AND PRACTICE OF AUTONOMY (1988).
22. For a valuable and relevant discussion, bearing particularly on means paternalism, see B. Douglas Bernheim & Antonio Rangel, *Beyond Revealed Preference: Choice Theoretic Foundations for Behavioral Welfare Economics*, 124 Q.J. ECON. 51 (2009).
23. Rebonato, *supra* note 6, is an especially helpful discussion.

that the best solution is for public officials to allow people to find their own path.

This is an argument about welfare, grounded in a claim about the superior information held by individuals. But there is an independent argument from autonomy, which emphasizes that even if people do not know what is best for them, and even if they would choose poorly, they are entitled to do as they see fit (at least so long as harm to others, or some kind of collective action problem, is not involved). On this view, freedom of choice has intrinsic and not merely instrumental value. It is an insult to individual dignity and a form of infantilization to eliminate people's ability to go their own way.[24]

Whether or not these objections to paternalism are convincing, my question here is whether and how they apply to people whose choice is not to choose. On reflection, they apply quite well, and this is why choice-requiring paternalism is no oxymoron. As we have seen, people might decline to choose for multiple reasons. They might believe that they lack information or expertise. They might fear that they will err. They might not enjoy the act of choosing; they might like it better if someone else decides for them. They might not want to incur the emotional costs of choosing, especially in situations that are painful or difficult to contemplate (such as organ donation or end-of-life care). They might find it a relief or possibly even fun to delegate.[25] They might not want to take responsibility. They might be too busy. They might be alert to their own biases. They might not want to pay the psychic costs associated with regretting their choice. Active choosing saddles the chooser with

---

24. For an illuminating and skeptical discussion, suggesting that overriding choices need not entail a lack of respect, see SARAH CONLY, AGAINST AUTONOMY: JUSTIFYING COERCIVE PATERNALISM 1–7 (2012).

25. See Cass R. Sunstein & Edna Ullmann-Margalit, *Second-Order Decisions*, 110 ETHICS 5 (1999).

responsibility for the choice and can reduce the chooser's welfare for that reason.

In daily life, people defer to others, including friends and family members, on countless matters and are often better off as a result. I have noted that in ordinary relationships, people benefit from the functional equivalent of default rules, some explicitly articulated, others not. In a marriage, for example, certain decisions (such as managing finances or planning vacations) might be made by the husband or wife by default, subject to opt-out in particular circumstances. That practice has close analogues in many contexts where people are dealing with private or public institutions and choose not to choose. We have seen that people may be willing to pay others a lot to make their choices for them. But even when there is no explicit payment or grant of the power of agency, people might well prefer a situation in which they are relieved of the obligation to choose because such relief will reduce decision costs, error costs, or both.

Suppose that Jones believes that he is not likely to make a good choice about his retirement plan and would therefore prefer a default rule, chosen by someone who is a specialist in the subject at hand. In Mill's terms: Doesn't Jones know best? Or suppose that Smith is exceedingly busy and wants to focus on her most important concerns, not on a question about the right health insurance plan for her or even about the right privacy setting on her computer. Doesn't Mill's argument support respect for Smith's choice? If policymakers accept that argument and care about people's welfare, they might well defer to the chooser's choice, even if that choice is not to choose. If freedom of choice is accepted on the ground that people are uniquely situated to know what is best for them, then that very argument should support respect for people's choices when they freely choose not to choose.

Or suppose that Winston, exercising her autonomy, decides to delegate decisionmaking authority to someone else and thus to relinquish the power to choose, in a context that involves health insurance, energy providers, privacy, or credit card plans. Isn't it an insult to Winston's dignity rather than a way of honoring it, if a private or public institution refuses to respect that choice?

It is at least plausible to suppose that respect for autonomy requires respect for people's decisions about whether and when to choose. That view seems especially reasonable in view of the fact that people are in a position to make countless decisions and might well decide that they would like to exercise their autonomy by focusing on their foremost concerns, not on what seems trivial, boring, or difficult.[26] They might believe that time is precious, and they might want to spend that most precious of commodities on other matters. They might want to focus on their real concerns; that is how they exercise their agency.

DO PEOPLE DISLIKE DEFAULTS? BEYOND REACTANCE

Some people think that default rules intrude into people's freedom, but the points just made throw that thought into considerable doubt. There is a related question, empirical in nature: Are people genuinely bothered by the existence of default rules, or would they be bothered if they were made aware that such rules had been chosen for them? I have referred to the phenomenon of *reactance*, which suggests that people can reject efforts to control their choices. Those very efforts can lead people's commitment to their original plan to grow stronger. If an authority figure encourages people not to smoke, there is a risk that such people will react

---

26. *See* Esther Duflo, *Tanner Lectures on Human Values and the Design of the Fight Against Poverty* (May 2, 2012), http://economics.mit.edu/files/7904.

by smoking even more. When people feel that their freedom is at risk, reactance becomes more likely. The idea of defiance captures an aspect of reactance and can threaten the effectiveness of well-meant interventions. To what extent is this a problem for default rules?

Researchers do not have a full answer to this question; the particular setting and the level of trust undoubtedly matter. We have seen that the phenomenon of "receptance" parallels that of reactance, as people sometimes welcome suggestions, defaults, and even constraints. A comprehensive empirical literature on receptance has yet to emerge, but it undoubtedly will. In the meantime, consider this finding in the context of end-of-life care: When people are explicitly informed that a default rule is in place and has been chosen because it affects people's decisions, that information has essentially no effect on what people do. Here's how the study worked.[27] Participants were provided with two defaults:

1. I want my health care providers and agent to pursue treatments that help me to live as long as possible, even if that means I might have more pain or suffering.
2. I want my health care providers and agent to pursue treatments that help relieve my pain and suffering, even if that means I might not live as long.

When one of these was the default, it was given to people as the preselected option, but they had the opportunity to check off a different alternative by entering their initials. As expected, people were

27. *See* George Loewenstein et al., Warning: You Are About to Be Nudged (2014) (unpublished manuscript, available at http://papers.ssrn.com/sol3/papers.cfm?abstract_id=2417383). For relevant discussion, see Gidon Felsen et al., *Decisional Enhancement and Autonomy: Public Attitudes Toward Overt and Covert Nudges*, 8 JUDGMENT AND DECISION MAKING 203 (2012).

far more likely to stick with the default. But a number of the participants were also informed as follows:

The specific focus of this research is on "defaults"—decisions that go into effect if people don't take actions to do something different. Participants in this research project have been divided into two experimental groups.

If you have been assigned to one group, the Advance Directive you complete will have answers to questions checked that will direct health care providers to help relieve pain and suffering even if it means not living as long. If you want to choose different options, you will be asked to check off different options and place your initials beside the different options you select.

If you have been assigned to the other group, the Advance Directive you complete will have answers to questions checked that will direct health care providers to prolong your life as much as possible, even if it means you may experience greater pain and suffering.

Notably, explicitly informing people in advance of all this did not have a significant effect on where they ended up; whether or not they were informed in this way, they were equally likely to stick with the default. There was no evidence of reactance. This finding strongly suggests that people may not be uncomfortable with defaults as such, even if they are told of their effects and are specifically informed that a particular default has been chosen because of those effects. Here, too, a usual response might be "yeah, whatever."

To be sure, the issue of end-of-life care is distinctive, and different results might be found in other settings where people might be more resentful of the default. In the context of organ donation, for example, people who are skeptical of the idea of "presumed consent" might be more likely to change the default if explicitly informed that opt-out was chosen because it increases the supply of organs for donation. More research would be highly desirable on this question and in particular on the circumstances in which default rules produce reactance, receptance, or no effect at all.

FREEDOM AND ITS ALIENATION

In some contexts, a choice not to choose might seem to be an alienation of freedom. In the extreme case, people might choose to be slaves or otherwise relinquish their liberty, in the sense of their choice-making power, in some fundamental way. A possible example: People might choose not to vote, not in the sense of failing to show up at the polls but in the sense of (formally) delegating their vote to others. Of course it is legitimate to consider what others think, but formal delegations are legally impermissible. One reason is that they would undo the internal logic of a system of voting, in part by creating a collective action problem that a prohibition on vote-selling solves: If everyone could sell his vote, many people might (rationally) do so, even if the result would be to create collective harm by concentrating political power in particular vote-buyers. The basic idea is that if vote-selling were permitted, voting power could be concentrated in individuals or individual entitles, and while decisions to sell might be individually rational, the result would be bad from the standpoint of a large group of vote-sellers. But an independent reason for prohibiting vote-selling is that individuals would be relinquishing their own freedom to select their leaders. Perhaps that relinquishment is unacceptable in itself.

Or perhaps people might choose not to make choices with respect to their religious convictions, or their future spouse, and they might delegate those choices to others.[28] In cases that involve central or intimate features of people's lives, we might conclude that freedom of choice cannot be alienated even voluntarily and that the relevant decisions must be made by the individuals themselves. We might think that because people know best about what suits them or their situation, a delegation is simply too risky, even if people want to delegate. Or we might think that in cases that involve the choice of a religion or a spouse, it is essential that people *take responsibility*. An abdication of responsibility might be inconsistent with the nature of religious conviction, properly understood. And if you have not chosen your own spouse, you might have a weaker commitment to the marriage. (This is of course an empirical matter, and cultures vary.) Recall as well the importance of authenticity. If the context is one in which it is important for people to make a choice that is authentically theirs, then they must not choose not to choose. That choice, or any kind of delegation, might be an objectionable refusal to exercise agency, resulting in outcomes that are not sufficiently one's own.

It is a complex question which cases involve a genuine alienation of freedom or an unacceptable surrender of authenticity. But even if the category is fairly large, it cannot easily be taken as a *general* objection to the proposition that on autonomy grounds, people should be allowed not to choose in multiple domains. Even if autonomy and agency require a sense of responsibility for intimate or defining choices, they do not do so for the wide range of cases in which people do not choose to choose and do not want to be bothered.

---

28. For relevant discussion, see Amitrajeet Batabyal, *On the Likelihood of Finding the Right Partner in an Arranged Marriage*, 30 J. Socio-Econ. 273 (2001); Conly, *supra* note 24.

CHOOSERS' INTERESTS

It bears emphasizing that the choice not to choose may not be in the chooser's interests (as the chooser would define it). For that reason, choice-requiring paternalism might have a welfarist justification. Perhaps the chooser chooses not to choose only because he lacks important information (which would reveal that a delegation or a default rule might be harmful) or suffers from some form of bounded rationality. A behavioral market failure might infect a choice not to choose, just as it might infect a choice about what to choose.

A nonchooser might, for example, be unduly affected by "availability bias" because of an overreaction to a recent situation in which her own choice went horribly wrong. Or perhaps the chooser is myopic and is excessively influenced by the short-term costs of choosing, which might require some learning (and so some investment), while underestimating the long-term benefits, which might be very large. Recall as well that a form of "present bias" might infect the decision not to choose. People might face a kind of *intrapersonal collective action problem*, in which such a decision by Jones at Time 1 turns out to be welfare-reducing for Jones at Times 2, 3, 4, and 5.

But for those who reject paternalism, these kinds of concerns are usually a justification for providing more and better information, rather than for blocking people's choices, including their choices not to choose. In these respects, the standard objections to paternalism apply as well to those who insist on active choosing. Of course it might be wrong to object to paternalism.[29] But with respect to their objections, an important question is whether the choice not to choose is, in general or in particular contexts, likely to go wrong. In the abstract, there is no reason to think that that

29. *See* CONLY, *supra* note 24.

particular choice would be especially error-prone. In light of people's tendency to overconfidence, the choice not to choose might even be peculiarly likely to be right, which would create serious problems for choice-requiring paternalism.[30]

WELFARE LOSSES AND BANDWIDTH NEGLECT

Consider in this regard evidence that some people spend too much time trying to make precisely the right choice, in a way that leads to significant welfare losses. In some situations, people underestimate the temporal costs of choosing but exaggerate the benefits, thus producing "systematic mistakes in predicting the effect of having more, vs. less, choice freedom on task performance and task-induced affect."[31] If people make such systematic mistakes, it stands to reason that they might well choose to choose in circumstances in which they ought not to do so, if their own welfare is what matters. In an important book, Barry Schwartz explores the multiple problems that people face when they have too many choices and the difficulty of solving those problems without a little help.[32] Schwartz argues that in some contexts, people would be better off with fewer choices. A closely related conclusion is that in many cases, people would do best to rely on a default rule.

There is also evidence that some of our behavioral biases are on full display when we are making decisions for ourselves, but are diminished or even invisible when we are making decisions for

---

30. *See* ULRICH HOFFRAGE, *Overconfidence, in* COGNITIVE ILLUSIONS: A HANDBOOK ON FALLACIES AND BIASES IN THINKING, JUDGMENT, AND MEMORY 235 (Rudiger F. Pohl ed., 2012).

31. *See* Botti & Hsee, *supra* note 4, at 161.

32. *See* BARRY SCHWARTZ, THE PARADOX OF CHOICE: WHY MORE IS LESS (2003).

others. It is for this reason that agents will sometimes make better decisions than principals—and for this reason as well that principals sometimes do well to rely on agents. It is imaginable that even when people suffer from unrealistic optimism with respect to their own prospects, they have an accurate sense of the probabilities when they are thinking about the prospects of other people. And in fact, Jennifer Arlen and Stephan Tontrup have found that agents do not display the "endowment effect," by which people value goods that they own more than they value the same goods when placed in the hands of others.[33] In a similar vein, Emily Pronin and her colleagues have explored "bias blind spots," which means that people are far more able to identify biases in others than in themselves.[34] For example, people detect self-serving biases in other people even as they fail to detect them in their own judgments.

There is a large implication here for choosing not to choose. If people are less biased when making decisions for others, then it may well make sense for them to ask (trusted) others to make decisions for them, or at least to provide a great deal of help. Of course it is true that if you are really blind to your own biases, you are unlikely to choose not to choose because of a desire to reduce the effects of biases. But many people, and many principals, have sufficient general awareness of their own propensity to error, and hence are willing to rely on formal or informal agents (doctors, lawyers, investment advisers, colleagues) for that reason.

I have emphasized that people suffer from limited bandwidth, which is one reason that they choose not to choose. But they also suffer from "bandwidth neglect," in the sense that they do not sufficiently appreciate their own bandwidth limitations. Bandwidth

33. See Jennifer Arlen & Stephan Tontrup, Does the Endowment Effect Justify Legal Intervention?: The Debiasing Effect of Institutions, 44 J. Legal Stud. (forthcoming).
34. See Emily Pronin et al., Bias Blind Spot: Perceptions of Bias in Self Versus Others, 3 Personality and Soc. Psychol. Bulletin 369 (2002).

neglect is closely related to and helps explain the "planning fallacy," which means that people typically think that they will complete tasks far more quickly than they actually do.[35] If people are alert to the limitations in their bandwidth, they will often choose not to choose—but if they suffer from bandwidth neglect, they will focus on problems and choose to choose when it really is in their interest to attend to other matters. To the extent that this is so, people choose to choose only because of some kind of mistake. Indeed, bandwidth neglect might count as a behavioral market failure. On this question as well, far more empirical work is needed.

My aim here is not to take a general stand on the legitimacy of paternalism, but only to say that the standard opposing arguments apply to all its forms, including those that interfere with the decision not to choose. I have emphasized that some people who care about human welfare are willing to interfere with people's choices; they may well be libertarian or nonlibertarian paternalists.[36] But on welfare grounds, the standard arguments on behalf of freedom of choice apply to those who (freely) choose not to choose. And from the standpoint of autonomy and dignity, interference with the choice not to choose seems objectionable as well, unless it is fairly urged that that choice counts as some kind of alienation of freedom and relinquishment of responsibility.

CASES

In which cases would it be paternalistic to reject a choice not to choose? Everything depends on the *reasons* why choice architects reject that choice.

---

35. For an overview, see DANIEL KAHNEMAN, THINKING, FAST AND SLOW 253–255 (2011).
36. *See* CONLY, *supra* note 24.

Begin with the case of punishing people for failing to choose. Suppose that people are subjected to criminal punishment if they do not choose—for example, for whom to vote or which health care plan to purchase. To know whether paternalism is involved, it is necessary to specify why it is that people are being required to choose. If people face some kind of collective action problem and coercion is meant to solve that problem, paternalism is not involved. For example, if the goal is to get everyone to contribute to the common defense or to the solution of an environmental problem, government is not acting paternalistically. But if public officials believe that people are erring from the standpoint of their own welfare if they do not choose, and are punishing people to ensure they do what is best for them, paternalism is involved.

Whether or not people should be forced to vote or purchase health insurance, there is a plausible argument that in both contexts, the goal of coercion is to solve a collective action problem. We have already explored that argument in the context of voting. For health care, the problem is that if people do not sign up for insurance, the rest of us are going to pay for their medical needs in any case; people are not going to be allowed to die. Compulsory insurance solves that problem. But it is easy to imagine cases where people are being forced to choose solely or partly on the ground that it is good for them to do so. At least some of those who support both compulsory voting and compulsory health insurance believe exactly that. In the latter context, the idea might be that people suffer from inertia and hence do not sign up, or because of unrealistic optimism or present bias, they fail to make a choice that will protect them in the event that things go unexpectedly wrong.[37]

---

37. In relation to inertia, see Punam Anand Keller et al., *Enhanced Active Choice: A New Method to Motivate Behavior Change*, 21 J. Cons. Psych. 376, 377–78 (2011).

Now turn to cases of leveraging, which seem to involve many of the most interesting problems. In those cases, some choosers undoubtedly have a second-order preference not to choose, and active choosing interferes with or overrides that preference. Nonetheless, choice architects are imposing a requirement of active choosing in circumstances in which some or many people, faced with the option, would choose not to choose. Is active choosing paternalistic for that reason?

As before, the answer turns on *why* choice architects are insisting on active choice. In the case of organ donation, paternalism is not involved. The goal is to protect third parties, not choosers. So, too, when choice architects favor default rules that reduce environmental harms; in such cases third parties are at risk. But suppose that as a condition for entering into an employment relationship, people are asked or required to make an active choice with respect to their retirement plan. Suppose, too, that choice architects believe that it is good for people to do so, even though prospective employees disagree (and would prefer to rely on a default rule). If so, those who insist on active choosing are hardly avoiding paternalism; they are engaging in it.

It might seem puzzling to suggest that paternalism might be involved in ordinary market settings. How can it be paternalistic to say that you have not purchased a pair of shoes, a cell phone, an automobile, or a fish sandwich unless and until you have actively chosen it, and said that you are willing to pay for it? The question is a good one, but it should not be taken as rhetorical; everything depends on the reasons that underlie the creation of a particular system of choice architecture.[38] To be sure, there are many justifications for

---

38. I am bracketing here the question whether markets can be seen as a kind of spontaneous order, or whether they should be seen as a product of conscious design. For a valuable discussion, see Edna Ullmann-Margalit, *Invisible Hand Explanations*, 39 SYNTHESE 263 (1978).

free markets and active choosing, and most of them have nothing to do with paternalism. Some of those justifications speak of efficiency and others of autonomy. But suppose you think that *active choosing is a way to ensure that people develop certain characteristics, values, and tastes.* Suppose you think that choosers gain independence, self-sufficiency, and a sense of agency and initiative, and that a system of active choosing is desirable for exactly that reason. That would be a paternalistic justification.

This view is hardly foreign to those who emphasize the importance of freedom of choice; it plays a significant role in Mill's own defense of liberty. This view is also a cousin of an early defense of free markets, memorably sketched by Albert Hirschmann, which emphasizes that free commerce creates a kind of culture in which traditional social antagonisms, based on religion and ethnicity, are softened as people pursue their economic interests.[39] For some of those who prize active choosing, the concern is not the softening of social divisions but the development of engaged, spirited, informed people.

I have noted that those who favor active choosing often embrace a form of liberal perfectionism, embodied in the idea that the government legitimately inculcates certain desirable characteristics on the ground that it is best for people to have those characteristics.[40] To the extent that active choosing promotes independence, self-sufficiency, and a sense of initiative, it might be preferred on perfectionist grounds, even if people would choose not to choose.

To be sure, it is not exactly standard to see those who embrace free markets as favoring any kind of paternalism. And it is often

---

39. *See* ALBERT HIRSCHMANN, THE PASSIONS AND THE INTERESTS (1997).
40. *See* JOSEPH RAZ, THE MORALITY OF FREEDOM (1986); liberal perfectionism is criticized by JOHN RAWLS, POLITICAL LIBERALISM (1991).

wrong to see them in that way, because other justifications are available and because people often do in fact have a first-order desire to choose. But suppose that private or public institutions favor active choosing, and reject mandates or default rules, because they want to influence people for their own good. Recall my working definition, which suggests that paternalism is involved when a private or public institution does not believe that people's choices will promote their welfare and is taking steps to influence or alter people's choices for their own good. If people have a second-order desire not to choose and active choosing overrides that choice, then paternalism is indeed involved.

WHICH TRACK?

Notwithstanding its potential benefits, active choosing could also create serious problems and is hardly the right approach in all situations. Often people benefit from not choosing. To see why, consider the words of Esther Duflo, one of the world's leading experts on poverty:

> We tend to be patronizing about the poor in a very specific sense, which is that we tend to think, "Why don't they take more responsibility for their lives?" And what we are forgetting is that the richer you are the less responsibility you need to take for your own life because everything is taken care of for you. And the poorer you are the more you have to be responsible for everything about your life.... Stop berating people for not being responsible and start to think of ways instead of providing the poor with the luxury that we all have, which is that a lot of decisions are taken for us. If we do nothing, we are on the

right track. For most of the poor, if they do nothing, they are on the wrong track.[41]

Duflo's central claim is that people who are well off do not have to be responsible for a wide range of things, because others are making the relevant decisions, and to their benefit. In countless domains, choices are in fact "taken for you," often by default rules or the functional equivalent. Such steps not only increase people's welfare but also promote their autonomy, because they are freed up to spend their time on other matters.

In well-functioning societies, people do not have to decide how and whether to make water safe to drink or air safe to breathe; they do not have to decide whether to build roads and refrigerators and airplanes; the Constitution settles the basic structure of the federal government, and citizens revisit that structure rarely if at all; the alphabet is given, not chosen. It is true and important that people may participate in numerous decisions through politics and markets. But often we are able to rely on the fact that choices are made by others, enabling us to go about our business without troubling ourselves about them. This is a blessing, not a curse.

BURDENS ON CHOOSERS

These points suggest a serious problem with active choosing, which is that it can impose large burdens on choosers. Suppose that the situation is unfamiliar and complicated. Suppose that people lack

41. Susan Parker, *Esther Duflo Explains Why She Believes Randomized Controlled Trials Are So Vital*, Ctr. for Effective Philanthropy (June 23, 2011), http://www.effectivephilanthropy.org/blog/2011/06/esther-duflo-explains-why-she-believes-randomized-controlled-trials-are-so-vital/ (alteration in original).

information or experience. If so, active choosing may impose unjustified or excessive costs on people; it might produce frustration and appear to require pointless red tape.

Most consumers would not much like it if, at the time of purchase, they had to choose every feature of their cell phone plan or all of their computer's initial settings. The existence of defaults saves people a lot of time, and most of those defaults may well be sensible and suitable. Few consumers would like to spend the time required to obtain relevant information and to decide what choice to make. As compared with a default rule, active choosing increases the costs of decisions, sometimes significantly.

In the process, active choosing can increase "decision fatigue," creating problems for other, potentially more important decisions.[42] Decision fatigue might make it difficult for people to focus on the central questions that affect their lives—tasks associated with their families, their jobs, their health, the well-being of their loved ones. Recall here the finding that the state of being poor, and focusing constantly on how to make ends meet, has a significant adverse effect on IQ, roughly equivalent to that of having no sleep the night before. Because people have limited bandwidth, it is no light thing to force them to pay attention to questions in which they have little interest, because that very requirement diverts scarce cognitive (and perhaps emotional) resources from other endeavors. It is in part because of cognitive scarcity that people choose not to choose. For the same reason, active choosing can be a serious imposition.

---

42. On decision fatigue, see *id.*; Jonathan Levav et al., *Order in Product Customization Decisions: Evidence from Field Experiments*, 118 J. POL. ECON. 274, 287, 290 (2010).

BURDENS ON PROVIDERS

At the same time, active choosing can impose large burdens on providers. The basic point is that defaults can be desirable and even important for those who supply goods or services. The reason is that defaults help providers avoid costs, which might result in increases in prices (and thus harm consumers as well).

Without a series of default rules and with constant active choosing, significant resources might have to be devoted to patient, tedious explanations and to elaborating the various options with consumers or users, who might not welcome the exercise. The experience of selling a cell phone, a car, or a laptop might be horrific if active choosing were required for every product characteristic. The same is true for retirement and health insurance plans. Many people are enthusiastic about the idea of financial education, but its track record is quite mixed, and sensible default rules might well be better.[43] It is easy to imagine a bit of science fiction or perhaps a situation comedy that would make this point especially vivid.

ERRORS

A final point, emphasized perhaps above all by those who prefer not to choose, is that active choosing can increase errors. A central goal of active choosing is to make people better off by overcoming the potential mistakes of choice architects. But if the area is unfamiliar, highly technical, and confusing, active choosing might have the opposite effect. If consumers are required to answer a set of technical questions, and if the choice architects know what they are doing,

---

43. *See* Lauren Willis, *The Financial Education Fallacy*, 101 AM. ECON. REV. 429 (2011).

then people will probably enjoy better outcomes with defaults. Perhaps it would be best to rely on experiments or pilot studies that elicit choices from informed people, and then to use those choices to build defaults. But if choice architects have technical expertise and are trustworthy, there is a question whether this exercise would be worthwhile.

A BRIEF ACCOUNTING

It should now be clear that a simple framework, investigating the costs of decisions and the costs of errors, provides a great deal of help in explaining when it makes sense to choose and when it makes sense to choose not to do so. That framework, focused on human welfare, is not complete; it cannot easily capture some important variables (such as the importance of agency and authenticity). But it does clarify the decisions of choosers and choice architects alike.

To the extent that the area is unfamiliar and confusing, default rules are desirable because they reduce both decision costs and error costs. But if choice architects are ignorant or biased, they will not be in a good position to devise accurate default rules, and to that extent there is an argument for active choosing. If the population of choosers is diverse, active choosing has real advantages because it diminishes error costs. By hypothesis, one size does not fit all. To the extent that preferences and situations change over time, there is a further argument for active choosing: any default rule may well become anachronistic. The value of learning and agency, and of the development of tastes and preferences, may well argue on behalf of active choosing as well—a general theme that has run throughout my discussion and that argues against choosing not to choose.

In view of these considerations, simplified active choosing has a great deal of appeal. Recall that under this approach, active choice is essentially the default, but people can reject it. For example, an institution might say: "We want you to choose your health care plan, but if you do not wish to do so, here is a default that, in our view, suits your needs." Sometimes this approach minimizes decision costs and error costs, and it can also be seen to protect people's autonomy as well (as a default rule, standing by itself, might not, simply because it tends to stick). These points should not be taken to suggest that simplified active choosing is the right approach for all times and places. Sometimes a default rule is better. But in many contexts, simplified active choosing is the best approach of all.

THIRD PARTIES

Throughout the discussion, I have been assuming that the welfare of choosers is all that matters, and that the choice between active choosing and a default rule is best assessed by reference to choosers' welfare. In many cases, of course, the interests of third parties are involved. Those interests complicate the analysis in two different ways.

EXTERNALITIES AND COLLECTIVE ACTION PROBLEMS

The first problem involves externalities. Return to the organ donation example. A choice architect might conclude that if the welfare of choosers is all that matters, active choosing is best. But suppose that with this approach, hundreds or even thousands of lives will be lost that would be saved with a default rule in favor of donation.[44] For that very reason, the choice architect might want to give serious consideration to that default rule, even if the case for active choosing would otherwise be quite strong.

Or consider the case of energy suppliers. Suppose that from the standpoint of the consumer, the best approach is to require active choosing among various providers, on the ground that different options (involving varying costs and varying environmental effects) will suit different people's values and situations. But suppose as well that greener energy sources would avoid significant environmental harms. If so, the argument for green defaults might be overwhelming. (Recall, however, that distributional considerations might be relevant. If poor people do not opt out and wealthy people do, a green default has a significant disadvantage.)

People might also face a collective action problem. With respect to public goods, including clean air, active choosers might produce a result that is far inferior to the result that would emerge if they could solve a coordination problem or a prisoner's dilemma. Of course social norms might have that same effect.[45] But often norms are insufficiently effective. In such cases, default rules might also be inadequate, because people can opt out, in which case the collective action problem will rematerialize, at least if a prisoner's dilemma is involved.

It is true that in the presence of externalities or a collective action problem, a mandate or ban might be justified, at least if it can be shown to maximize net benefits. When externalities are real and significant, we have a standard market failure, calling for

---

44. See Eric Johnson & Dan Goldstein, Do Defaults Save Lives, 302 SCIENCE 1338 (2003). I am not taking a stand on that issue here. In many nations, active choosing is indeed better, not least because family members will not take presumed consent to be authoritative.

45. See EDNA ULLMANN-MARGALIT, THE EMERGENCE OF NORMS (1976).

regulation that goes well beyond a default rule. But suppose that the externalities are not entirely clear, or that the obligations of choosers are complex and contested (as in the organ donor case), or that there are political obstacles to the use of mandates or bans. If so, a default rule, designed to address the likely externalities, might well be preferable to active choosing. A default rule might also be helpful in the case of collective action problems, certainly if coercion is unavailable. In the face of a problem of coordination, a default rule might be enough to do the trick. And in view of the power of inertia, a default rule might go some way toward solving or at least reducing a prisoner's dilemma.

PSYCHOLOGY, RESPONSIBILITY, AND CHOICE

The second point involves the potentially profound *psychological* differences between active choosing and defaults. Active choosing offers distinctive signals and has a distinctive meaning to both choosers and others. I have noted that with an active choice, the chooser takes full responsibility, and his intended decision is unambiguous. With a default rule, by contrast, both responsibility and intention can be murkier.[46] Other people might not quite know what the chooser wants, because inertia and inattention might be

---

46. *See* Bartling & Fischbacher, *supra* note 2. The authors find: "If the dictator delegates the decision right and the delegee makes the unfair choice, then mainly the delegee is punished, while the dictator is almost spared....By conducting treatments with and without punishment opportunities of the receivers, the experimental design allows to test whether the avoidance of punishment is indeed a motive for the delegation of a decision right. This is strongly confirmed as the share of delegated decisions is three times higher in the treatment with punishment than in the treatment without punishment opportunities." *Id.* at 69.

responsible for his apparent decision (which may be no decision at all). This difference matters.

Recall the phenomenon of "choice bias," which means that people show a strong preference for options they have actually chosen over equally good options they have not actually chosen.[47] As noted, people choose what they like, but they also like what they choose.[48] This point has implications for thinking about the differences between active and passive choices. There is reason to think that if people have made an active choice, they will become invested in it and in a sense like it (more), and that the same effects will not occur when the choice has been made passively and by default.

Imagine that the goal is to promote healthy behavior or to increase the likelihood that people will act in ways that promote the public interest (for example, by reducing pollution or threats of crime). If they make those choices actively, they are likely to be committed to them, and that commitment might have desirable spillover effects, perhaps by spurring other such decisions. But if people make those choices by default, their own preferences have neither been registered nor affected. These points may not be decisive in favor of active choosing, but they do suggest a potential downside to defaults.

Or to take a related issue: Suppose that someone is defaulted into being an organ donor or into a "no heroic measures" approach toward extension of her own life. In such circumstances, a responsible family member might well hesitate before honoring the relevant "choices," for exactly the same reasons that mandate the use

47. *See* Jeffery Cockburn et al., *A Reinforcement Learning Mechanism Responsible for the Valuation of Free Choice*, 83 NEURON 1 (2014).
48. *See* Tali Sharot et al., *Do Decisions Shape Preferences? Evidence from Blind Choice*, 21 PSYCHOL. SCI. 1231 (2010).

of quotation marks around that word. If what is sought is a clear expression of the chooser's actual will, and if other people will not take any apparent decision as authentic without such an expression, then there is a strong argument for active choosing—and thus for choice-requiring paternalism.

There are associated questions of guilt and regret, and these may argue either for or against active choosing. Suppose a family member is herself deciding whether to take heroic measures to extend the life of someone she loves. If choice architects—the government, the medical profession, a hospital—require her to make an active choice, her responsibility is clear; it is hers alone. If, by contrast, a default rule goes one way or the other, she can reasonably rely on or refer to it, serving to diffuse her responsibility and also carrying a kind of authority that influences her choice. She might well appreciate such effects; she might not want to assume responsibility. In fact it is sometimes said that in the context of end-of-life decisions, default rules can have exactly this effect. In France, family members have been said to be more comfortable with such decisions than in the United States—in part because a default rule operates in France more strongly than in the United States, and thus diminishes the sense of personal responsibility.

At the same time, it is easy to imagine settings in which the responsibility should be placed fully in the chooser's hands, partly to protect third parties, whole systems, or individuals themselves. Return to the case of voting, where a default rule would be objectionable in part because it intrudes on that responsibility. Where it is desirable to create a sense of responsibility, active choosing becomes far more appealing.

PART III

THE FUTURE

[6]

PERSONALIZATION

We have seen that some default rules are highly personalized. Such approaches draw on available information about which approach best suits different groups of people, and potentially each individual person, in the relevant population. In the future, private and public institutions will inevitably produce far more in the way of personalization, as large data sets and information about what particular people have chosen in the past greatly increase the level of accuracy.

THE BEST OF BOTH WORLDS?

It is possible to imagine a continuum of personalized approaches from the most fine-grained to the far more crude. In principle, choice architects could design default rules for each and every person on the planet. You could have your own default rule, and so could your best friend, and so could your worst enemy, and so could everyone in your neighborhood. In fact, every person could have a lot of default rules, each fitting the particular context—travel preferences, retirement plans, magazines, newspapers, health care plans, restaurant options, vacations, tablets, cell phones, household goods, and much more.

This idea may seems far-fetched, the stuff of science fiction. Indeed, the engaging 2013 science fiction movie *Her* plays with the idea of personalized defaults, even for romantic partners. The male lead, played by Joaquin Phoenix, falls in love with an operating system named Samantha, who seems to know exactly what he likes and defaults him into those things. She appears to be his perfect personalized partner. She knows what he wants, and she designs herself so that she *is* what he wants. It's just a movie, to be sure, and most of us are not going to fall in love with an operating system. But in the fullness of time, private and public institutions are likely to be able to use a large number of personalized default rules, and even if people do not fall in love with them, they will probably like them a lot.

In fact, technology is rapidly heading in that direction. Smartphone data can be (and has been) mined to ascertain personality traits, and those traits can in turn be used to personalize services on smartphones.[1] Many institutions use website browsing data to personalize a range of services, suggestions, and default options. Google, Netflix, and Facebook are only a few prominent examples. In many contexts, it is possible to move from active choosing to personalized default rules, as choice architects build such defaults for individuals on the basis of some combination of large data sets, demographic characteristics, and knowledge of what they have actively chosen in the past.

In their ideal form, personalized default rules might be thought to produce the best of both worlds—to capture what is attractive about both default rules and active choosing. Like impersonal default rules, personalized defaults reduce the burdens of decisions and simplify life. But like active choosing, they

---

1. *See generally* Gokul Chittaranjan et al., Mining Large-Scale Smartphone Data for Personality Studies (Oct. 14, 2011) (unpublished manuscript), *available at* http://publications.idiap.ch/downloads/papers/2011/Chittaranjan_PUC_2012.pdf (analyzing the relationship between behavioral characteristics derived from smartphone data and certain self-reported personality traits).

increase accuracy by tailoring outcomes to particular circumstances and thus overcoming the many problems associated with one-size-fits-all approaches.

Of course, the idea of personalized default rules raises serious concerns. Some of these involve narrowing our horizons; others involve the exercise of autonomy; others involve identification and authenticity; still others involve personal privacy. I shall turn to those concerns in due course. But at least in some contexts, the design of such personalized rules would be a great boon, promoting people's welfare and increasing their freedom. The key advantage of such rules is that they are likely to be more fine-grained and thus beneficial than "mass" default rules. As technology evolves and information accumulates, it is becoming increasingly easy to produce highly personalized defaults based on people's own choices and situations. For this reason, there will be promising opportunities to use default rules to make people's lives better in multiple ways. Such rules can make life not only simpler and more fun but also longer and healthier.

I have noted that every day, family members and friends use the equivalent of personalized default rules. They tend to know what people like in various domains. They do not ask, in every case, for an active choice, which would make life more complicated and potentially even intolerable. Sometimes spouses order for one another at restaurants or select clothing for each other, using the functional equivalent of default rules and pursuant to an implicit delegation. Sure, their choices may be inaccurate; we have seen that people make a lot of mistakes when choosing gifts, even for their spouses and close friends. Nonetheless, a large part of what it means to be a spouse, a partner, or a close friend is to be able to identify personalized defaults—to anticipate comforts, joys, and pleasures in advance. By contrast, strangers, and people on first dates, rely on impersonal ones, which may cause big trouble.

Especially as technology develops, an important function of marketing and marketing research will be to gather knowledge of this kind (subject to safeguards for privacy). Indeed, such marketing and research are becoming standard fare. Similar efforts are being made in political campaigns, with something close to the functional equivalent of personalized defaults in the form of online presentations to people who are most likely to be influenced by them. You might well find yourself, even now, receiving email solicitations, or online suggestions, that are personalized in the sense that they grow out of what someone, or some program, has managed to learn about you.

NOT QUITE THE BEST OF BOTH WORLDS?

Notwithstanding their many virtues, personalized default rules are not without disadvantages, even putting privacy to one side. Most obviously, they do not allow for agency and learning. They do not promote and may even impede the development of informed preferences. Return to the context of health insurance. People might be defaulted into a plan that suits their particular needs, which seems unobjectionable—but if so, they will not have the opportunity to learn, which might prove important in the long term. Perhaps it is best to require active choosing, so that people will come to know more about health insurance and their health care needs. Even personalized default rules do not provide the kinds of identification that come from one's own active choices.

Or consider the analogy of books and music. We have seen that on the basis of your past choices, it is possible, indeed easy, to offer advice or even suggest defaults that reflect what you like. If you have liked books by a certain mystery writer or science fiction writer, there is a good chance that you will like books by other identifiable mystery writers or science fiction writers. If you have liked music by certain singer-songwriters, companies can identify other singer-songwriters whom you will enjoy; this is how the website Pandora works its magic.

But we have also seen that people's preferences change over time, especially if they are able to learn, and when people are defaulted into options that simply reflect their current "likes," such learning will not occur. Recall the difference between an *architecture of control* and an *architecture of serendipity*. With an architecture of control, you are able to control what you see and hear. You make your choices, and the system reflects those choices. With an architecture of serendipity, life is full of surprises. You do not control what you see and hear. Great cities are full of serendipity. You encounter people, buildings, stores, products, art, and more, even if you would never have selected them in advance. You might find some of them jarring, even unpleasant, but they might change your day and even your life.

Pandora reflects the architecture of control. The same is emphatically true of personalized default rules in general. After those rules are in place, it is essentially goodbye to serendipity (unless one's personalized default rules makes space for surprises). But in multiple domains, serendipity has great value, as people learn and grow from encountering activities and products that do not in any way reflect their past choices. The problem, in short, is that if defaults are based on such choices, the process of personal development might be stunted. When your experiences are closely tailored to your past choices, your defaults are personalized, which is highly convenient, but you will also be far less likely to develop new tastes, preferences, and values.

In the context of communications generally, many people have expressed concern about the risks associated with an architecture of control in which people create a kind of "Daily Me"—an informational universe that is entirely self-selected.[2] Imagine, for example, that people are able to use perfect filters so that they can see and hear what they want and exclude everything else. If they have no interest in foreign affairs, they can restrict their reading to their own nation. If they prefer certain political views, they can restrict themselves to people who have those views. If they want to focus on sports, they can focus only on sports. All of us could devise a Daily Me for our particular tastes. In one variation, people could make a single choice or small set of choices, after which they would receive, by default, communications that fit their preferences and values. In some ways, this would be a great benefit, and because people evidently like it, the lived experience of many citizens does appear to be moving in this direction.

These are points about how people can filter on their own. But those who sell products and services can filter, too, and as they learn more about you, they can do so with increasing precision and default you accordingly, developing a Daily You.[3] In fact, personalized default rules are in a sense a kind of Daily You. Sellers could, if they learned about your past choices, provide you, very much in the style of Pandora, with other things that you might want to see, hear, or have. On this approach, the sellers' method of selection would be based on projections from your past choices. They might know that if you like certain kinds of shoes you will probably like other, similar kinds of shoes and perhaps certain socks and shirts as well, and maybe certain music, and perhaps even political candidates. This, too, might be a great boon. But insofar as it ensures a kind

---

2. Cass R. Sunstein, Republic.com 2.0 94 (2007); Eli Pariser, The Filter Bubble: How the New Personalized Web Is Changing What We Read and How We Think (2012).

3. See Joseph Turow, The Daily You: How the New Advertising Industry Is Defining Your Identity and Your Worth (2013).

of narrowing, and makes it less likely that people will expand their horizons, it has a serious downside.

Insofar as they involve culture and politics, personalized "echo chambers," in which people encounter only those views and ideas with which they already agree, threaten to produce both individual and social harm.[4] The individual harm comes from an absence of learning; self-narrowing can stunt people's development. The social harm comes from potential polarization, as people end up divided from one another in large part because they are listening only to people with whom they agree or at least have sympathy. From the individual and social points of view, an architecture of serendipity has large advantages over an architecture of control, because it ensures that people will come across all sorts of things they did not specifically select. Those things expand people's horizons and potentially change their lives, even if they never would have placed them in their Daily Me and even if no one would have placed them in their Daily You. Here, then, is a serious problem with personalized defaults, at least in some domains.

Return in this regard to a genuinely extreme case: a political system with personalized voting defaults, so that people are automatically defaulted into voting for the candidate or party suggested by their previous votes (subject of course to opt-out). In such a system, people would be presumed to vote consistently with their past votes to such an extent that they need not show up at the voting booth at all, unless they wanted to indicate a surprising or contrary preference. If you voted for the Democratic Party candidates four years ago, or eight, or twelve, you would find yourself voting for Democratic candidates for life, at least unless you opted out—not because you have specifically concluded that you want to do that in

4. See generally CASS R. SUNSTEIN, GOING TO EXTREMES 2 (2008) (explaining that "[w]hen people find themselves in groups of like-minded types, they are especially likely to move to extremes.").

individual cases, but because that's your personal default. In fact, it would be easy to construct a system of data mining, producing an algorithm able to specify, with considerable accuracy, how you would vote, or indeed how everyone would vote, so that no one would actually need to vote. In principle, the algorithm might be able to do people's voting for them.

Odd and terrible as it might seem, a system of default voting would not entirely lack logic. As already noted, it would certainly reduce the burdens and costs of voting, especially for voters themselves, who could avoid a trip to the polls, assured that the system would register their preferences. And in some ways, it would not be so radically different from the current system in which voters can, after all, engage in party-line voting (so long as they show up).

But we have also noted a (devastating) problem with a default voting system of this kind, which has to do with what might be called the internal morality of voting. The very act of voting is supposed to represent an active choice, in which voters are engaged, thinking, participating, and selecting among particular candidates. Of course this is an ideal, and far from a reality for everyone. If voters want to disengage or not to vote or to vote without thinking a lot, they certainly may, and they may also rely on simple cues (such as party affiliation). But the aspiration is important. With default voting, the level of active engagement would undoubtedly decrease, and automaticity could become a kind of norm. This is why default voting is not acceptable.

In most other contexts, there is not an equivalent internal morality, but active choosing is an individual and social good precisely because it promotes learning over time and thus the development of informed, broadened, and perhaps novel preferences, tastes, and values. Whenever this is the case, the standard objections to default rules are not weakened merely because the default rule is personalized. In some ways, those objections are even strengthened.

IDENTIFICATION, MOTIVATION, AND FUN

Personalized default rules have other disadvantages. We have seen that people tend to stick with the default, and this is true whether it is impersonal or personalized. Sticking with the default can lead to feelings of real regret. There is empirical support for this proposition: In the context of retirement plans, those who passively stay with the default show more regret than those who engage in active choosing.[5] It is at least a modest point for active choosing if regret is likely to be less intense.

A far more important point follows: passive choice will, almost by definition, decrease people's feelings of identification with the outcome. In part for that reason, any kind of default rule, including a highly personalized one, may not create the kinds of motivation that can spur desirable conduct and are most likely to follow from active choosing. When people have made an active choice, the outcome is authentically theirs in a way that it cannot be with even a highly personalized default. That point may well have behavioral consequences.

Suppose that choice architects seek to promote healthy behavior. In daily life, food choices are often automatic; within limits, people tend to eat whatever is in front of them. Aware of this point, and concerned about people's health, choice architects might use something akin to default rules of certain kinds—enlisting, for example, small portion sizes and easy availability of healthy foods in order to reduce obesity. Such an approach might be effective, and so there is a lot to be said for it. It might also be personalized, in the sense of being designed so as to fit people's particular situations.

5. *See* Jeffrey R. Brown et al., *The Downside of Defaults* (Nat'l Bureau Econ. Res., Working Paper No. 12-05, 2012), *available at* http://www.nber.org/aging/rrc/papers/orrc12-05 .pdf.

But it might not have the distinctive benefits associated with active choosing, which include increasing self-monitoring and strengthening people's intrinsic motivations. If the goal is to ensure that people are actively engaged in promoting their own health, and if active engagement will have cascading effects on their lives, then active choosing might well be preferable.

It is true and important that on this count, personalized default rules are better than impersonal ones. People might understand the former to reflect some kind of agency on their part, at least if the defaults are based on a reasonable or accurate judgment about their own preferences and desires. But because a personalized default rule is not a product of an actual choice, people are less likely to feel identified with it than they would with a genuine choice of their own.

A separate objection applies to personalized default rules no less than impersonal ones: Some people affirmatively favor a situation in which they receive a number of options and can make their own selections from the list. Whenever people like to choose, there is an argument for active choosing and against any sort of default rule. It is reasonable, and not false, to answer that if they want to choose, they can do so even in the presence of a default. But for many people in many contexts, it is better to be presented with a menu of options and be asked for their preference than to be provided with a default and be asked whether they want to depart from it.

There are also points about dignity, agency, and self-management. On those counts, personalized default rules may well be inferior to active choosing. Especially when the stakes are large, it might be best for people to make their own choices and not to rely on a default rule even if it is well-suited to their circumstances. In the case of marital choices, there is a strong argument to this effect, and such choices are not, in this respect, unique. Where decisions involve defining or intimate aspects of people's lives, a personalized default rule may turn out to be too comfortable, because it does not involve a real exercise of the power of agency.

ABSTRACTIONS AND CONCRETE CASES

These various points—about narrowing, regret, chooser identification, valuing the experience of choice, and agency—have force in some contexts but not in others. They should not be taken as decisive points against personalized default rules. It is right to worry about a narrow communications universe produced with the help of personalization. But it is much less clear that anyone should worry a lot about highly personalized defaults for retirement plans, health insurance plans, travel plans, or credit card plans. In all of these cases, learning may or may not be important, but personalization (so long as it is accurate) does not appear to threaten individual or social harm, or to endanger agency and dignity in any serious way.

More generally, personalized default rules may have benefits that dwarf the costs, even when the costs are real. While such defaults do not have all of the advantages of actual choosing, they have many of them, and at the same time they promise to overcome most of the problems associated with impersonal defaults. Above all, they can handle the problem of heterogeneity and thus accurately reflect preferences, without imposing the burdens and costs associated with active choosing.[6] To know whether the objections

6. Special questions might be raised by the potential creation of "personalized prices." Typical price systems name a single price for a good or service, even though people who are subject to that price would be willing to pay widely varying amounts for precisely the same items. Smith might be willing to pay far more than Jones for the same tablet or meal, perhaps because Smith is wealthier or because Smith has stronger preferences. The various questions raised by the possibility of personalized prices deserve a separate discussion.

are persuasive, it is necessary to investigate the particular context, not to adopt a general attitude of distrust toward personalized defaults.

TRACKING AND EXTRAPOLATING

A personalized default might be based on people's own past choices or on those of people "like them." Consider, for example, Amazon, which provides recommendations to its customers on the basis of their past choices. Amazon knows that if customers like books by a certain author, they will probably like books by another author as well. Amazon does not exactly create default rules, but it does produce visible, salient choices, based on personalized knowledge. Of course the presentation of such choices is akin to advice and not literally a default, in the sense that if customers do nothing, they will purchase nothing. But the same technologies could easily be used to create defaults of multiple kinds.

Once enough information is available about Smith, choice architects could design default rules for Smith with respect to health insurance, privacy, rental car agreements, computer settings, and so on. For some services, including travel, personalized defaults have become familiar and common. If a website knows where customers like to sit on an airplane, when they like to travel, which airlines they prefer, and how they like to pay, it can use this information to generate outcomes (subject to customer revision). "Prepopulation" of forms, and personalization of websites, can be terrific time-savers, and they do involve defaults.

Personalized default rules can also be dynamic, in the sense that they can change over time. In principle they could incorporate new information in real time. The best default rules or settings for a particular person in one year might be very different from those in the next year; age matters. Indeed, the default rules could change on a daily or even hourly basis. As private and public institutions receive increasing amounts of information about individuals, this project is becoming increasingly feasible. Multiple websites are already moving in this direction, providing defaults for people based on their own past choices. In general, these defaults make life simpler and more convenient.

We can imagine a large variety of possibilities here. In some cases, personalized defaults might be based directly on people's own past choices. Return to the travel setting: If you make certain choices in the past, you will be defaulted into the same choices in the future. In other cases, defaults might involve a degree of extrapolation from those choices. Choice architects might think that if people have made certain choices with respect to privacy in the domain of health insurance, they are likely to make certain choices with respect to privacy in other domains as well. If they like privacy in one context, they might well like it in another. Consider the familiar idea that if certain consumers actually like certain products, they will like certain other products as well. If sufficient data is available, personalized default rules might be generated in this way.

INFORMATION ACQUISITION AND PRIVACY

Feasibility. With respect to personalized defaults, one challenge involves feasibility. For defaults to be personalized, choice architects must obtain relevant information. In some contexts, obtaining such information is essentially costless. People make repeated choices on websites, and if choice architects know what people usually choose, they can make that usual choice the default. Return to the case of travel preferences, or consider shipping times and credit cards for book purchases.

But in other cases, there will be no such track record, at least at the beginning, and acquisition of relevant information will be costly or perhaps impossible. Suppose that people are purchasing new computers, and the question is the appropriate privacy setting for them. Choice architects might lack the necessary information. Personalized default rules might not be feasible. Perhaps choice architects could rely on large data sets, and in particular on "what people like you" have chosen. If so, the question is whether they can produce sufficiently accurate defaults. A form of simplified active choosing might be the best solution.

Privacy. Even when personalization is feasible, there is an additional challenge: If defaults are based on people's past choices, there might be a serious concern about privacy. By hypothesis, choice architects are identifying and relying on people's past choices, and some choosers will not be exactly delighted by that fact. People might well object if others know that they tend to like (say) silly romance novels—and they might be especially displeased to find that for that reason they are being defaulted into a wide range of choices favored by people who like such novels.

We should draw a distinction here. First, certain choice architects—those who operate relevant programs or websites—might simply know about people's past choices; if people are visiting their sites or purchasing goods from them, such knowledge would seem inevitable (though there may be retention issues).[7] Second, and alternatively, the choice architects who are receiving that information as a result of commercial interactions (or perhaps as a result of mere browsing) might take the further step of revealing those

7. One safeguard for privacy might include the nonretention of information after a specified period of time. Perhaps people could be asked to indicate their preferences (that is, make an active choice with respect to retention), or perhaps people could be subject to an impersonal (for example, retention unless indicated otherwise, or vice versa) or a personalized default.

choices to independent people and providers. On one view, such revelations would facilitate beneficial interactions, so people should enthusiastically welcome them. Companies can offer you goods or services you might well like. But it is easily imaginable that many choosers would object to sharing and revelations of this kind. Perhaps they do not want their purchases, or their browsing habits, to be shown to other providers (or to the commercial world). If they do object, perhaps sharing of that kind should not be permitted, and people should be allowed to ensure that it does not occur. The problem is that a prohibition on sharing will make it harder to generate personalized defaults.

There is a potential solution to the privacy problem. When privacy really matters, choice architects might use, *with respect to privacy itself*, either (1) active choosing or (2) personalized default rules. Perhaps choice architects should ask Jones explicitly about her preferences with respect to privacy. If they learn that Jones wants her privacy to be protected, then they should provide her with privacy-protective defaults. Or perhaps choice architects already know that Jones is fiercely protective of her privacy and that in the face of any kind of doubt, she does not want other people to know about her behavior and her choices. If so, that very knowledge can be used to produce privacy-protective default rules for Jones.

In the case of doubt, active choosing might be selected, so that people do not give up genuine and significant privacy interests unless they explicitly state their willingness to do so. With respect to privacy, there is a great deal of heterogeneity in the population, and there is also a risk of self-interested judgments on the part of choice architects. Both of these points argue for active choosing.

Demographics. Less ambitiously, personalized default rules might be based on group characteristics, such as geographic or demographic variables. For example, age and income might be used in determining appropriate default rules for retirement plans. In fact, this approach is already standard practice. For example, universities typically default faculty members into what seems to be an appropriate plan for them (subject of course to an easy opt-out). With respect to employees over sixty, the default allocation should be different from what it is with respect to employees under forty. For those with large incomes, the default might be different from what it would be for those with smaller incomes. The general idea is that your default rules would track what would be best for "people like you."

Evidence suggests that for retirement plans, default rules that respect diversity (especially with respect to age) are indeed feasible and can increase the probability of enrollment in the default plan by as much as 60 percent.[8] Default rules can also create very large gains for participants.[9] Life-cycle and life-stage funds do exactly this and are increasingly common. It is easy to imagine similar approaches to health insurance, credit cards, cell phones, mortgages, and much more. Of course, there might be constraints on the use of certain demographic variables—such as race, religion, and gender—if they would run afoul of principles of nondiscrimination.

The general points should not be obscure. Many of the strongest arguments against default rules and in favor of active choosing emphasize the potential inaccuracy of defaults. If the choice architect blunders, there can be real harm, and choosers may be less likely to blunder, if only because default rules tend to be crude. With

---

8. See Gopi S. Goda & Coleen F. Manchester, *Incorporating Employee Heterogeneity into Default Rules for Retirement Plan Selection* 29 (Nat'l Bureau Econ. Res., Working Paper No. 16099, 2010), *available at* http://www.nber.org/papers/w16099 (studying the effects on retirement plan choices when the default plan is altered based on participant age).

9. See *id.* ("Substantial welfare gains are possible by varying defaults by observable characteristics.")

personalized default rules, this problem can be greatly reduced. In many ways, personalization makes people freer by default. Personalized default rules are not exactly the best of both worlds. In some contexts, active choosing is indeed best, because it promotes learning and agency. But personalized defaults have a great deal of appeal, because they reduce the costs of decisions while also reducing the costs of errors. They are the wave of the future, and while that is not an unmixed blessing, it is mostly good news.

[7]

YOURS BY DEFAULT?

Predictive Shopping

We have seen that in free markets, people generally do not obtain goods and services unless they choose them. In that domain, active choosing is the rule. But why, exactly, is this so? Why is active choosing required? I have sketched an obvious answer: Unless people have actually said that they want some good or service, there is no way to know what they want and when they want it. No planner can possibly have the requisite knowledge.

Active choosing and the resulting freedom are, on this view, indispensable safeguards against error, understood as mistaken judgments about what people want. If, for example, a bookseller presumes that certain consumers want certain books, and defaults them into ownership (subject to opt-out), there would be an undue risk that people would end up with books that they do not want. It is true that people have to make decisions, which can be costly and burdensome, but requiring active choosing in ordinary markets minimizes the sum of decision costs and error costs. Recall Hayek's remarkable suggestion that "the awareness of our irremediable ignorance of most of what is known to somebody [who is a planner] is *the chief basis of the argument for liberty*." The planner is inevitably ignorant, and so should opt for liberty.

DATA-FIED YOU

To test these claims, consider a thought experiment, signaled above, in which sellers know, with perfect or near-perfect certainty, what people would want to buy. Suppose that large data sets, accompanied by information about people's past choices, help to ensure that level of accuracy. Suppose that on the basis of such data, a bookseller knows, with certainty or close to it, what people will buy before they know themselves. If so, the conclusion seems clear, at least if the goal is to promote people's welfare: People should be defaulted into those purchases. Of course excessive spending is a potential result, but if so, that very risk should be taken into account by the relevant data sets, which should be able to impose the kinds of spending limits that people want.

With these assumptions, "the chief argument for liberty" has been sufficiently answered. With the help of massive amounts of data, the default approach reduces (and even eliminates) decision costs and, by hypothesis, has zero or near-zero error costs. Under the thought experiment, people will get exactly what they want. It is tempting to object that such defaults, leading to a form of "predictive shopping," are unacceptable from the standpoint of autonomy, but the temptation should be resisted. I am speaking of cases in which a person or institution is able to know, with perfect or near-perfect certainty, what people want. If autonomy is what matters, is there a real problem? In such cases, sensible people might choose not to choose, because the default serves them perfectly well. It gives them what they want without requiring them to take annoying, unnecessary, or burdensome steps to obtain it.

This is a thought experiment, but of course the market is rapidly moving in a direction of this kind. Any account will soon be out of date, but consider a few examples by way of illustration. Walmart has adopted a mobile app with a form of predictive shopping.[1] The app analyzes what a particular customer ordinarily purchases, and by means of that analysis compiles a list that the customer sees on opening the app. The goal is to anticipate what customers will like and need. According to a Walmart official, "the best shopping list is the one you don't have to create, so that's the one we're working on." In his view, "the future of retailing is the history of retailing, of a personalized interactive experience for every customer delivered through a smartphone."

Through Amazon subscriptions, you can subscribe to periodic shipments of laundry supplies, cereals, baby care products, pet supplies, vitamins, soap, shampoo, candy, and much more. To be sure, you have to sign up, and you make the judgments about what and when. But the principle is the same. Numerous people have signed up.

In the same general vein, Freshub, an Israeli startup, "makes it super easy to organize your shopping and ensure your kitchen is always stocked with your favorite items."[2] The basic goal is to eliminate the need to choose groceries by establishing a series of defaults based on previous purchases. Many other companies are providing related services. Trunk Club allows men to sign up to see a stylist who takes information about their style and body type and mails them a customized selection of clothes (not on a regular basis, but on request). Stitch Fix has a similar service for women's clothing—except there is a fee for the style consultation. There will be far more in this vein in the future.

---

1. Stephen Lawson, *Wal-Mart to Send Automated Shopping Lists to Its Mobile App*, TechHive (May 22, 2013, 2:20 PM), http://www.techhive.com/article/2039564/walmart-to-send-automated-shopping-lists-to-its-mobile-app.html; *Walmart to Add Automatic Shopping Lists to Its Mobile App*, RetailCustomerExperience.Com (May 28, 2013), http://www.retailcustomerexperience.com/news/walmart-to-add-automatic-shopping-lists-to-its-mobile-app/.

2. Freshub, http://www.freshub.com/clients/ (last visited Oct. 15, 2014).

SURVEYS

To test reactions to predictive shopping, I conducted a number of surveys. I began by asking about seventy Harvard University students (in law, business, and public policy) the following question:

> *Suppose that over the years, your favorite online bookseller has compiled a great deal of information about your preferences. It thinks it knows what you want before you do. Would you approve or disapprove if the seller decides in favor of "default purchases," by which it sends you books that it knows you will purchase, and bills you (though you can send the books back if you don't want them)? (Assume that the relevant algorithm is highly reliable—accurate in at least 99 percent of cases—though not completely unerring.)*

Notably, 84 percent disapproved. Perhaps the objection is that the bookseller is enrolling people automatically and without their consent. But in a separate survey, the same people were asked whether they would voluntarily sign up for such a program. In that case, a large majority—70 percent—would also decline. True, the difference between 84 percent and 70 percent is significant. With respect to predictive shopping, the difference suggests that if they are given an opportunity to sign up, people will react more positively than if they are automatically enrolled. An approval rate of 30 percent is not exactly low. If a company could convince 30 percent of a large population of people to sign up to receive books through some kind of predictive algorithm, it would be doing very well. But even with voluntary sign-up, participation was well under 50 percent.

With a different population, recruited for Amazon Mechanical Turk, I found broadly similar results. Of fifty people, 86 percent rejected default purchases, and 84 percent would decline to sign up.

I followed these surveys with a more formal one involving a nationally representative sample with five hundred respondents (with an error rate of plus or minus 4.5 percent). The questions were similar to those in the surveys just reported, with some changes for clarity. The setup was this:

> *Suppose that over the years, your favorite online bookseller has compiled a great deal of information about your preferences. On the basis of a new algorithm, it thinks it knows what you will want to buy before you do. Assume that the relevant algorithm is highly reliable—accurate in more than 99 percent of cases, in the sense that it chooses to send people books that they will, in fact, want to buy.*

Here is the first question:

> *Would you choose to enroll in a program in which the seller sends you books that it knows you will purchase, and bills your credit card? (Assume that you can send the books back, with a full refund, if you don't want them, and that you can always say that you no longer want to participate in this program.)*

Forty-one percent of people said yes and 59 percent said no. This result is noteworthy for two different reasons. First, most people want to make their own choices and would decline to enroll (as in the other surveys). But 41 percent would sign up (a significantly higher number than in the other surveys). It is striking, and perhaps a signal of the future, that over two-fifths of a nationally representative group of people were willing to participate in such a program.

The second question asks about automatic sign-up:

> *Would you approve or disapprove if the seller automatically, and without your explicit consent, enrolls you in a program in which*

it sends you books that it knows you will purchase, and bills your credit card? (Assume that you can send the books back, with a full refund, if you don't want them, and that you can always say that you no longer want to participate in this program.)

Twenty-nine percent said that they would approve and 71 percent said that they would disapprove. This is a statistically significant difference from the first question; it supports the view that people would be more likely to sign up for a system of automatic purchases than to approve of a situation in which a seller signs them up without their explicit consent. Nonetheless, it is noteworthy that 29 percent—nearly a third—would approve.

WHY?

These results are a bit of a puzzle, because at first glance, the most serious problems with predictive shopping, and with the resulting defaults, involve accuracy—and in the question, a high level of accuracy was stipulated. How can the survey results be explained?

Distrust. One possibility is that people did not believe the stipulation. In the real world, of course, there is a risk that those who use the relevant algorithms will be self-serving. They want to sell their products, and they might assume a desire to purchase even when people lack, or would not form, that desire.

To be sure, competitive markets will discipline errors of this kind, and people should be able to return products that they do not want—but because of the power of inertia, many people will not bother to do so and will retain unwanted products.[3] When people

---

3. Robert Letzler & Joshua Tasoff, *Everyone Believes in Redemption: Overoptimism and Defaults* (Working Paper, 2013), *available at* http://papers.ssrn.com/sol3/papers .cfm?abstract_id=2066930.

reject the idea of default purchases or predictive shopping, it may be because they distrust the incentives of the seller and do not believe that firms should be allowed to profit from inertia.

Search as benefit, search as cost. Another explanation for the results is that in the distinctive context of book-buying, many people actually enjoy the opportunity to search among options, to find out what has arrived, to see what's new, to thumb through pages, and to choose accordingly. Search is a benefit rather than a cost. If so, automatic book purchases are not exactly wonderful. They eliminate much of the fun. Compare the case of a college student who has to trudge off to the bookstore to purchase books that are required for classes. Such a student might well be happy, not sad, if the books magically appeared in her room at her dormitory. If it's obligatory to buy specific books, it's not a benefit to have to go out and get them.

Or consider the process of ordering taxicabs. If some kind of algorithm knew exactly when you will need a cab and could ensure that the cab will be there for you exactly when you need it, then the automatic arrival of a cab would be highly desirable. The only question would be the accuracy of the algorithm; if it really works, who would not want to benefit from it? Searching for a taxi, or ordering one, has none of the appeal of searching for a terrific new novel.

The general lesson is that the appeal of predictive shopping, or automatic purchases, depends in part on whether search is a cost or a benefit. Books are not of course unique. For many people, it is really fun to try to find just the right vacation, or hotel, or tennis racquet, or suit or shirt or dress, or partner or spouse. To the extent that this is so, automaticity eliminates a valuable activity. An analogy: Some behavioral research finds that people particularly enjoy *experiences,* and that if you want to spend your money in a way that will improve your subjective well-being, you will buy vacations, not commodities.[4] In some domains, choosing is itself an experience and one that people like. For such people, default rules would be a big mistake.

Changing preferences. There is another problem with predictive shopping, which is that people's preferences change over time, certainly with respect to books, vacations, and clothing. We have seen that what people want this month might be quite different from what they want next month and the year after, when predictions are being made. People might like Stephen King novels in June but have little interest in them in January, and predictive shopping algorithms might well have a difficult time capturing such changes. If purchases are automatic, changes in preferences will not even register, because people will not be buying actively and thus signaling those changes. Even if the algorithms are extraordinarily good, they must extrapolate from the past, and the extrapolation might be hazardous if people do not like in the future what they liked in the past, or if they like in the future what that they did not like in the past.

ARE ROUTINE PURCHASES DIFFERENT?

It is of course an empirical question, not a conceptual one, whether and to what extent changing preferences would confound predictive shopping. Perhaps the relevant predictions would be perfectly accurate, or nearly so, across certain domains. Perhaps the algorithm could even predict changing preferences. And with respect to certain household items—soap, toothpaste, toilet paper—preferences do not much change, and automatic purchases at the time of need could be a great boon.

4. *See* ELIZABETH DUNN & MICHAEL NORTON, HAPPY MONEY (2013).

Imagine a kind of household manager that would automatically supply, at a charge, certain products as soon as people run out. What would be wrong with that? I asked about seventy Harvard University students the following question:

> Assume that at some point in the future, homes can be monitored so as to "know" when you run out of various goods, such as soap, paper towels, and toilet paper. Would you approve of a system in which the home monitor automatically buys such goods for you, once you run out?

The strong majority—69 percent—did indeed approve. It is noteworthy that in these surveys, people's negative reactions to predictive shopping "flipped," compared to books, when household items were involved. One reason may be that for such items, tastes are relatively static and errors are unlikely. Unlike in the context of book-buying, it is also not exactly a benefit, for most people, to choose among items of this kind. And in the event of some kind of error, people might not much mind the idea of having extra soap, paper towels, and toilet paper. Compare automatic renewal of newspapers or magazine subscriptions, which many people welcome.

Notably, a different population, recruited on Amazon Mechanical Turk, did not approve of automatic shopping even in the context of household goods; there was no "flipping" in that context. In a group of fifty people, only 38 percent were in favor. Perhaps people were skeptical about the neutrality and accuracy of the home monitoring system. Participants might have feared that the monitor would buy goods that people did not want or need. We have seen that skepticism about choice architects, or about household monitors, can lead people to favor active choosing, even if choosing is not exactly fun. And perhaps the members of this population did not much mind shopping. It is imaginable that Harvard students are unusually unenthusiastic about spending their time looking for household goods.

The same basic result came in a survey of a national representative sample, whose members were asked a similar question:

> *Would you approve or disapprove of a system in which the home monitor automatically, and without your explicit consent, buys such goods for you, once you run out, and bills your credit card? (Assume that you can send the goods back, with a full refund, if you don't want them, and that you can always say that you no longer want to participate.)*

Only 32 percent would approve, whereas 68 percent would not. Both figures are noteworthy. The fact that almost a third of respondents would approve of such a system suggests that for household goods, predictive shopping has a lot of potential. And the fact that Harvard students were more enthusiastic about the idea might be a product of age; young people might well be especially comfortable with technologies that "shop" for them.

With the nationally representative sample, responses did not greatly change when people were asked whether they would voluntarily enroll in a program of this kind:

> *Would you choose to enroll in a program in which the home monitor automatically buys such goods for you, once you run out, and bills your credit card? (Assume that you can send the goods back, with a full refund, if you don't want them, and that you can always say that you no longer want to participate.)*

Only 38 percent would enroll, while 62 percent would not. Here as elsewhere, the majority's refusal to participate is worth underlining, especially because it is not a lot of fun to purchase the relevant goods. Perhaps people did not trust those who would run the program.

But it is again worth underlining the fact that a significant minority (nearly two-fifths) would enroll. The difference is statistically significant. There was a real "bump" in favor of the program when participation was voluntary rather than presumed.

Recall that something like the hypothesized home monitor is now available. The subscription services offered by Amazon do not monitor your home, but they do send you what you think you need on the basis of the timing you specify. Once you enroll, you receive products periodically through a system that is analogous to automatic credit card or mortgage payments.

THE MATRIX

In light of these findings, consider a two-by-two matrix of different sorts of purchases:

	Easy or automatic	Difficult and time-consuming
Fun or pleasurable	Impulse purchases (candy, magazines, some clothes)	Books, trips and vacations, cars
Not fun or pleasurable	Household staples (toilet paper, soap, toothpaste)	Retirement plans, health insurance

For cases in the upper left quadrant, choosing imposes low decision costs, and making the relevant choice is a benefit, not a cost. In such cases, there is little reason for predictive shopping. The active choice is a large part of the point. By contrast, the upper right quadrant involves difficult choices—but for many people it is a benefit to make those decisions. In such cases, a lot of people will not want predictive shopping, because it would take away the fun.

The lower left quadrant is an excellent setting for predictive shopping, because people do not enjoy the activity. But the costs of choice are low, so there is not an urgent need for automaticity. Whether it is worthwhile depends on whether people would greatly benefit from saving the relevant time. (Recall the difference between Harvard students and the general population on this count.) For predictive shopping, the lower right quadrant is the most important one. In such cases, making a choice is not fun or pleasurable, and because choosing is hard, there would be real value in automaticity. If predictive shopping could be made accurate and easy, there would be a good argument for automatic purchases. It is in this context that predictive shopping could deliver real benefits. Other categories of purchases that could fall in this quadrant include household items that are replaced infrequently (light bulbs, batteries, and unusual kinds of sheets and towels).

It is important to emphasize that what falls in which quadrant will vary from person to person. For some people, the lower right quadrant would include shopping for clothes, while for others, that form of shopping might well fall in the upper left or upper right. Shopping for a car is fun for many people but unpleasant and even a bit traumatic for many others. For some people, making investment decisions is difficult but somehow rewarding, even fascinating, and so preparing for retirement is not something that they would like to avoid. For other people, automaticity would be a great boon. Consider the revealing words of President Barack Obama: "You'll see I wear only gray or blue suits. I'm trying to pare down decisions. I don't want to make decisions about what I'm eating or wearing. Because I have too many other decisions to make."[5]

5. Quoted in Michael Lewis, *Obama's Way* (Oct. 12, 2012), *available at* http://www
.vanityfair.com/politics/2012/10/michael-lewis-profile-barack-o.

SOLUTIONS

If the empirical problems could be solved, so that accuracy were not a problem, many people would be better off with predictive shopping, at least for cases in the bottom quadrants. If so, it might even make sense to assume that people would prefer it and would choose not to choose. The most forceful objection is that in many domains, the empirical problem cannot be solved—at least not yet. The principal qualification, signaled by the matrix, is that automatic enrollment in programs of this kind would not be a good idea where people actually enjoy making selections.

In these circumstances, the appropriate solution seems simple. As a general rule, people should not be defaulted into a system of predictive shopping, but they should be given an opportunity to make an active choice about whether they want to enroll. Sometimes the risk of error is very low. Some algorithms prove themselves over time, and some people will want to take their chances with them even if they have not been proved. Such consumers will think: "I do not want to bother to shop; the seller knows me well enough to choose for me." Other consumers will think: "I enjoy shopping; it is a benefit rather than a cost; and I don't trust the seller."

In short, people should be making active choices about whether they want to enroll in programs that increase automaticity. In making those choices, people should beware of inertia and procrastination, which may prove serious obstacles to participation in beneficial programs. The time they save will be their own.

[8]

COERCION

Default rules preserve freedom of choice. Even though those who embrace active choosing tend to be suspicious of such rules, they acknowledge the importance of allowing people to opt out. But in light of behavioral findings demonstrating the occasional human propensity to blunder, some people have been asking whether mandates and bans have a fresh justification.[1] The motivation for that question is clear: If people's choices lead them in the wrong direction, is it really best to maintain freedom of choice? In the face of human errors, isn't it odd or even perverse to insist on that form of freedom? Isn't it especially odd to do so if it is clear that in many contexts, people choose not to choose?

If a mandate would clearly increase social welfare, there is a strong argument on its behalf. Of course it would be necessary to specify what social welfare means, and human dignity and agency matter.[2] But we can identify many cases where mandates make sense, especially but not only if harm to others is involved. In the

---

1. *See* SARAH CONLY, AGAINST AUTONOMY (2012); Ryan Bubb & Richard Pildes, *How Behavioral Economics Trims Its Sails and Why*, 127 HARV. L. REV. 1593 (2014).

2. Freedom of choice is, on any reasonable account, an important ingredient in social welfare. *See* Daniel J. Benjamin et al., *Beyond Happiness and Satisfaction: Toward Well-Being Indices Based on Stated Preference*, 104 AM. ECON. REV. 2698 (2014); Björn Bartling et al., *The Intrinsic Value of Decision Rights* (U. of Zurich, Dep't of Econ. Working Paper No. 120, 2013), *available at* http://papers.ssrn.com/sol3/papers.cfm?abstract_id=2255992. For a valuable discussion of foundational issues, see Matthew Adler, WELL-BEING AND FAIR DISTRIBUTION: BEYOND COST-BENEFIT ANALYSIS (2011).

face of such harm, or some kind of collective action problem, a mandate or a ban, or an economic incentive, may be required. No one believes that defaults are a sufficient approach to the problem of violent crime. No one thinks that people should be allowed to choose whether to steal or to assault; in such contexts, prohibitions are perfectly appropriate, even in the freest of free societies. In the face of a standard market failure, coercion has a familiar justification; consider the problems of occupational safety or air pollution. And if there is a distributional problem, nations might not be able to rely on either active choosing or default rules; redistribution is the ordinary solution (with the progressive income tax usually being the appropriate mechanism).

It is true that even in the face of market failures or distributional problems, defaults may have an important role. Recall the possibility of default rules in favor of clean energy, which can significantly reduce the market failures that give rise to air pollution. When mandates are not feasible, default rules can help, and even when mandates are in place, default rules can increase compliance. Such rules might also be designed to promote distributive goals, as in the case of opt-in requirements designed to protect poor consumers from inadvertently incurring late fees and overuse charges, and "direct certification" of eligibility for school meals, defaulting poor children into programs providing free breakfasts and lunches. But the effects of defaults, taken by themselves, might well prove too modest when there are significant externalities or collective action programs, and they hardly exhaust the repertoire of appropriate responses.

We have seen that there are behavioral market failures as well. If people are suffering from unrealistic optimism, limited attention, or a problem of self-control, and if the result is a serious welfare loss for those people, there is an argument for some kind of public response, possibly in the form of a mandate. When people are running high risks of mortality or otherwise ruining their lives, it might make sense to coerce them. After all, people have to get prescriptions for certain kinds of medicines. Even in freedom-loving societies, people are prohibited from buying certain foods or running certain risks in the workplace, simply because the dangers are too high. We can certainly identify cases in which the best approach is a mandate or a ban because that response is preferable, from the standpoint of social welfare, to any alternative, including defaults.

FIVE OBJECTIONS TO MANDATES

Nonetheless, there are good reasons to think that if improving social welfare is the goal, and if dignity and agency matter, defaults have significant advantages and are often the best approach. I have identified those reasons as grounds for favoring active choosing over defaults, but they have even more force if invoked on behalf of defaults as opposed to mandates or bans.

First, freedom-preserving approaches tend to be best in the face of heterogeneity. By allowing people to go their own way, defaults reduce the costs associated with one-size-fits-all solutions, which mandates typically impose. We have seen that in the context of credit markets, some people benefit from overdraft protection programs, even if the interest rates are high. Forbidding such enrollment or sharply limiting people's access to such programs could turn out to be harmful. For credit cards and mortgages, people have different tastes, situations, and needs, and because they allow opt-in or opt-out, default rules have large advantages over prohibitions. To be sure, personalized defaults can reduce the problems posed by heterogeneity, but it can also be challenging to devise them.

Second, those who favor defaults are alert to the important fact that public officials have limited information and may themselves err (the knowledge problem). If defaults are based on mistakes, the damage is likely to be significantly less severe than in the case of mandates, because people are free to ignore them. True, defaults can be sticky, but we have seen that many people opt out when they really do not like them. Return once more to the instructive example of default thermometer settings in winter: If they are set 1°C colder, people stick with them, but if they are set 2°C colder, the default is a lot less sticky. The example shows that people will reject a default if it makes them uncomfortable—an important safeguard against inadequately informed choice architects. Here again, the rise of large data sets and personalized default rules can reduce the problem, but one would have to be quite optimistic to think that they can eliminate it.

Third, defaults respond to the fact that public officials may be affected by the influence of well-organized private groups (the public choice problem). Even if such officials have a great deal of knowledge, they might not have the right incentives, even in well-functioning democracies. Powerful private groups might want particular defaults, and sometimes they can convince officials to endorse what they want. If so, the fact that people can go their own way provides real protection, at least when compared with mandates.

Fourth, defaults have the advantage of avoiding the welfare loss that people experience when they are deprived of the ability to choose. In some cases, that loss is severe. As we have seen, people sometimes want to choose, and when they are forbidden to do so, they might be frustrated, angered, or worse. A default avoids that kind of loss.

Fifth, defaults recognize that freedom of choice can be seen and often is seen as an intrinsic good, which government should respect if it is to treat people with dignity and respect. Some people believe that autonomy and agency have independent value and are properly taken as part of human dignity, rather than as merely one of a large category of goods that people enjoy. If people are deprived of freedom, they are infantilized. It is true that defaults can be challenged on the same ground, but at least they allow people to go their own way if they like. It is not necessary to enter into difficult philosophical territory in order to agree that these points support defaults over mandates.

Some people object that defaults are more covert and less transparent than mandates, and therefore more insidious and difficult to monitor. If so, there would be a distinctive argument against defaults. But if defaults are transparent and publicized, as they (always) should be, the objection is misplaced. Defaults need not be, and ought not to be, covert. Manipulation must be avoided, and nothing should happen behind people's backs. There is nothing covert or manipulative about automatic enrollment in savings and health insurance plans. (Recall that unless active choosing is required, some kind of default rule is inevitably in place.) And while it is true that many people may not pay attention to default rules or understand their effects, recall the evidence that people's behavior in the face of a default would not be changed even if they were informed that a particular default, and not another imaginable one, has been chosen for them.[3]

ILLUSTRATIONS

These arguments in favor of choice-preserving approaches will have different degrees of force in different contexts. They suggest reasons to favor defaults over mandates, but those reasons

3. *See* George Loewenstein et al., Warning: You Are About to Be Nudged (2014) (unpublished manuscript).

may not be decisive. In some settings, for example, the interest in freedom of choice has overwhelming importance. In others, people do not much care about it, and its intrinsic value is only modest. I have emphasized that in the face of externalities or collective action problems, defaults may be insufficient, and that there is a place for mandates when the goal is redistribution or fairness. Consider three illustrative problems, in increasing order of complexity.

1. Suppose that a large university has long had a single-sided default for its printers and is deciding whether to change to double-sided. On the basis of careful investigation, suppose that it has learned that at least 80 percent of its students, faculty, and other employees would prefer a double-sided default on the ground that they would like to save paper. Armed with this information and aware of the economic and environmental savings that a double-sided default could bring, the university switches to that default.

Now suppose that some university administrators, enthusiastic about the idea of majority rule, ask whether double-sided printing should be mandatory. The answer to that question is plain. About one-fifth of users prefer a single-sided default, and there is little doubt that single-sided printing is often best—for example, for PowerPoint presentations and for lecture notes.

The assessment might be different if the use of single-sided printing imposes significant costs on nonusers (for example, paper costs on the university or environmental costs). If so, there is some weighing to be done; in some cases, externalities do tip the balance. But if the welfare of those who use printers is the only or primary variable (and it would seem to be here), a default is clearly preferable to a mandate. From the standpoint of users, a mandate would impose unnecessary costs in the face of heterogeneity across persons and projects. Here, then, is a clear case in which a default is preferable to a mandate.

2. We have seen that a great deal of work has explored the effects of automatic enrollment in retirement plans. We have also seen that automatic enrollment increases participation rates, and thus people's savings, while also preserving freedom of choice. So far, so good. The problem is that if the default contribution rate is lower than what employees would choose (say, 3 percent, as it has been under many automatic enrollment plans) then the result of automatic enrollment might be to *decrease* average savings, because the default rate turns out to be sticky.[4] This is an ironic result for those who want to use defaults to increase people's welfare during retirement.

The natural response, however, is not to abandon default rules in favor of mandate, but to choose a better default. One possibility is "automatic escalation," which increases savings rates each year until the employee hits a predetermined maximum.[5] In fact, there has been a significant increase in the use of this approach; automatic escalation is increasingly popular.[6] Another possibility is to select a higher default contribution. No one denies that

4. *See* Bubb & Pildes, *supra* note 1.
5. Shlomo Benartzi & Richard H. Thaler, *Behavioral Economics and the Retirement Savings Crisis*, 339 Science 1152 (2013). Bubb and Pildes, *supra* note 1, note that the typical maximum contribution rate even after automatic escalation may still be too low, but this problem, too, can be accommodated within libertarian paternalism by simply raising the maximum contribution rate.
6. In 2009, 50 percent of plans with automatic enrollment included escalation; by 2012, 71 percent did. *See* Employers Expressing Doubt in Retirement Readiness of 401(k) Plan Participants, Towers Watson Survey Finds, *available at* https://www.towerswatson.com/en/Press/2012/10/employers-expressing-doubt-in-retirement-readiness-of-401k-plan-participants.

defaults can go wrong.[7] If they do, the challenge is to get them right.

But there is a more fundamental objection, which questions freedom of choice altogether—not because of externalities or collective action problems, but because of a behavioral market failure. Suppose that people opt out of pension plans for bad reasons, in the sense that the decision to opt out makes their lives go worse (by their own lights). Perhaps the relevant people have a general (and unjustified) distrust of the financial system, or of their employer, and so they elect to save little or not to save at all. Perhaps they suffer from an acute form of present bias. Perhaps those who opt out are most likely to suffer as a result of doing so.

These are empirical questions, but if so, the argument for a mandate gains force on welfare grounds. If public officials really know, from practice, that a behavioral market failure, or some kind of error, is leading people to make self-destructive blunders, it is tempting to contend that government should mandate savings and eliminate the right to opt out. After all, most democratic nations have mandatory pension plans of one kind or another, and perhaps they should expand those plans rather than working to allow or encourage voluntary supplementation. Indeed, some critics might argue for some kind of comprehensive welfare assessment by public officials about optimal savings rates and ask those officials to build mandates on the basis of that assessment.

This approach cannot be ruled out in principle, but there are good reasons for considerable caution. In assessing the rationality of the choices of those who opt out, public officials might be wrong (recall the knowledge problem). As compared to a default,

---

7. Note the important finding that default-induced improved choices, at the level of individuals, can undermine social welfare by substantially exacerbating adverse selection. *See* Benjamin Handel, *Adverse Selection and Inertia in Health Insurance Markets: When Nudging Hurts*, 102 AM. ECON. REV. 2643 (2013).

a mandate would get people into the system who would benefit from inclusion, but it would also get people into the system who would be seriously harmed. It is important, and it may be difficult, to know the size of the two groups. Those who opt out might do so not for bad reasons, or because they are ignoring their future selves, but because they need the money now and are making a sensible trade-off between their current and future welfare.

To say the least, a comprehensive welfare assessment of optimal savings rates is exceedingly difficult, especially in view of the diversity of the population and changes over time. What is the right savings rate for those who are twenty-five, or thirty, or forty, or sixty? And how does it change when people have to pay school loans or mortgages or pay for their children, young or old? And how does it change for people who earn $30,000 per year, or $60,000, or $100,000? And how do changing macroeconomic conditions affect the situation?

Any such assessment would have to acknowledge that different approaches make sense for different people and over time. In a recession, for example, a lower contribution rate might make more sense, at least for relatively low-income people, than in a time of growth. So, too, those who have to pay off their college loans might not want to save much while they are struggling to make those payments, and people who are reasonably spending a great deal on current consumption (perhaps they have young children or children in college) might not want to save a lot in that period. These points suggest the need for personalized rather than one-size-fits-all mandates, which would not be easy to design and would amount to a risky form of social engineering.

Moreover, any form of coercion will impose a welfare loss on at least some choosers who would want to exercise their autonomy and would undoubtedly be frustrated to find they cannot. And if freedom of choice has intrinsic value or can promote learning, then there are further reasons to avoid mandates.

These various points raise serious cautionary notes about mandates and bans. True, they might not be decisive. As I have noted, many nations compel savings through some kind of social security program, and for perfectly legitimate reasons. Perhaps existing programs should be expanded to increase the level of mandatory savings. If it could be demonstrated that those who opt out are making genuinely bad decisions, there would be a strong argument for mandates (or at least for altering rules that reduce the risk of harm). But even if so, private retirement plans have an important place for savers, and the question is whether the current voluntary system should become more coercive. The fact of heterogeneity and the risk of government error argue strongly in the direction of defaults.

3. Most motor vehicles emit pollution, and the use of gasoline increases national dependence on foreign oil. On standard economic grounds, there is a market failure, and some kind of corrective tax (and no mere default rule) seems the best response, designed to ensure that drivers internalize the social costs of their activity. Behaviorally informed regulators would be inclined to add that at the time of purchase, many consumers do not give sufficient attention to the costs of driving a car. Even if they try, they might not have a sufficient understanding of those costs, because it is not simple to translate differences in miles per gallon into economic and environmental consequences. An obvious approach, preserving freedom of choice, would be disclosure, in the form of a clear, simple fuel economy label that would genuinely inform people and so correct that kind of behavioral market failure. And in fact, the Obama administration produced a label of exactly that kind.[8]

8. *See* Cass R. Sunstein, Simpler (2013).

But it is reasonable to wonder whether such a label will be sufficiently effective. Perhaps many consumers will pay little attention to it, and so will not purchase cars that would save them a significant amount of money. True, a corrective tax might help solve that problem, but if consumers really do neglect fuel costs at the time of purchase, it might be best to combine the tax with some kind of subsidy for fuel-efficient cars, to overcome consumer myopia. And if consumers are genuinely inattentive to the costs of operating a vehicle (at the time of purchase), then it is possible that sensible fuel economy standards, which are not favored on standard economic grounds, might themselves turn out to be justified. Here, too, policymakers may well be justified in considering a mandate (and of course fuel economy mandates have become common in many nations).

In support of that argument, it would be useful to focus directly on two kinds of consumer savings that result from fuel economy standards and do not involve externalities at all: money and time. In fact, the vast majority of the quantified benefits from recent fuel economy standards come not from environmental improvements but from money saved at the pump. Turned into monetary equivalents, the time savings are also significant. For the most recent and ambitious of those standards, the Department of Transportation found consumer economic savings of about $529 billion; time savings of $15 billion; energy security benefits of $25 billion; carbon dioxide emissions reductions benefits of $49 billion; other air pollution benefits of about $14 billion; and somewhat less than $1 billion from reduced fatalities.[9] The total projected benefits are $633 billion over fifteen years, a remarkable 84 percent of which comes from savings at the pump, and no less than 86 percent of which comes from those savings along with time savings.

9. Nat'l High. Traf. Safety Administration, *Final Regulatory Impact Analysis: Corporate Average Fuel Economy for MY 2017–MY 2025*, August 2012, table 13.

The problem is that on standard economic grounds, it is not at all clear that policymakers are entitled to count these consumer benefits in the analysis, because they are purely private savings and do not involve externalities in any way. In deciding which cars to buy, consumers can certainly take account of the private savings from fuel-efficient cars; if they choose not to buy such cars, it might be because they do not value fuel efficiency as much as other vehicle attributes (such as safety, aesthetics, and performance). Where is the market failure? If the real problem lies in a lack of information, the standard economic prescription overlaps with the behaviorally informed one: *Provide that information so that consumers can easily understand it.*

In this context, however, there is a risk that any kind of choice-preserving approach will be inadequate. Even with the best fuel economy label in the world, consumers might well be insufficiently attentive to those benefits at the time of purchase, not because they have made a rational judgment that those benefits are outweighed by other factors, but simply because they focus on other variables.[10] How many consumers really think about time savings when they are deciding whether to buy a fuel-efficient vehicle?

This question raises a host of empirical questions, to which full answers are not yet available. But if consumers are not paying enough attention to savings in terms of money and time, a suitably designed fuel economy mandate—hard paternalism and no mere default—might turn out to be justified, because it would produce an outcome akin to what would be produced by consumers who were at once informed and attentive. If the benefits of the mandate greatly exceed the costs, and if there is no significant consumer welfare loss (in the form, for example, of reductions in

---

10. *See* Xavier Gabaix & David Laibson, *Shrouded Attributes, Consumer Myopia, and Information Suppression in Competitive Markets*, 121 Q.J. Econ. 505, 511 (2006).

safety, performance, or aesthetics), then the mandate does serve to correct a behavioral market failure. And indeed, the U.S. government has so argued:

> The central conundrum has been referred to as the Energy Paradox in this setting (and in several others). In short, the problem is that consumers appear not to purchase products that are in their economic self-interest. There are strong theoretical reasons why this might be so:
>
> — Consumers might be myopic and hence undervalue the long term.
> — Consumers might lack information or a full appreciation of information even when it is presented.
> — Consumers might be especially averse to the short-term losses associated with the higher prices of energy-efficient products relative to the uncertain future fuel savings, even if the expected present value of those fuel savings exceeds the cost (the behavioral phenomenon of "loss aversion").
> — Even if consumers have relevant knowledge, the benefits of energy-efficient vehicles might not be sufficiently salient to them at the time of purchase, and the lack of salience might lead consumers to neglect an attribute that it would be in their economic interest to consider.
> — In the case of vehicle fuel efficiency, and perhaps as a result of one or more of the foregoing factors, consumers may have relatively few choices to purchase vehicles with greater fuel economy once other characteristics, such as vehicle class, are chosen.[11]

11. Light-Duty Vehicle Greenhouse Gas Emission Standards and Corporate Average Fuel Economy Standards; Final Rule, Part II, 75 Fed Reg 25,324, 25,510–11 (May 7, 2010), *available at* http://www.gpo.gov/fdsys/pkg/FR-2010-05-07/pdf/2010-8159 .pdf.

Of course regulators should be cautious before accepting a behavioral argument on behalf of mandates or bans. Behavioral biases have to be demonstrated, not simply asserted; perhaps most consumers do pay a lot of attention to the benefits of fuel-efficient vehicles.[12] The government's numbers, projecting costs and benefits, might be wrong; recall the knowledge problem. Consumers have highly diverse preferences with respect to vehicles, and even though they are not mere defaults, fuel economy standards should be designed to maximize flexibility and to preserve a wide space for freedom of choice. The use of fleet-wide averages helps to ensure that such space is maintained, because it allows room for a diverse array of vehicles.

With these qualifications, the argument for fuel economy standards, made by reference to behavioral market failures, is at least plausible. In this context, nudges (in the form of an improved fuel economy label) and mandates (in the form of standards) might march hand in hand. With an understanding of behavioral findings, a command-and-control approach, promoting consumer welfare, might turn out to be far better than the standard economic remedy of corrective taxes. And in this context, default rules and active choosing are hardly enough.

LESS RISKY

The fuel economy example is important, but it should not be read for more than it is worth. It certainly does not establish that in the face of human error, mandates are *generally* preferable to choice-preserving alternatives. We have seen that such alternatives,

---

12. Hunt Allcott & Michael Greenstone, *Is There an Energy Efficiency Gap?*, 26 J. ECON. PERSP. 3 (2012).

above all active choosing and defaults, reduce the high costs of imposing solutions on heterogeneous populations; reduce the serious risks associated with government error; avoid the many costs associated with eliminating freedom of choice; and are more protective of individual autonomy, agency, and dignity. In light of the frequently unanticipated and sometimes harmful effects of mandates, default rules are generally less risky.

No one should deny that in the end, mandates might turn out to be justified on social welfare grounds. But in a free society, it makes sense to start and usually to end with less intrusive, choice-preserving alternatives, at least when a standard market failure is not involved.

CONCLUSION

Free by Default

I began this book by noting that more than at any other point in human history, it is possible to ask people this question: *What, exactly, do you choose?* Both public and private institutions can obtain answers to that question, even in real time. With respect to music, computers, books, cell phones, privacy, movies, television shows, retirement planning, health insurance, newspaper stories—you can be asked to choose what you want, today, tomorrow, next week, and next year. In effect, you can establish the settings for the furniture of your life. And if you have not changed your settings in a while, or today, you can be asked, every day or every week, whether you would like to do so. You can even choose how often you would like to be asked. Human beings are newly free to exercise their own agency.

The problem is that time and attention are limited, and whenever people ask you to make a choice, they are imposing on you. Often people dislike those impositions. They choose not to choose, or they would do so if asked—and sometimes they prefer not to be asked.

For those who choose not to choose, the good news is that more than at any point in human history, choice architects, or social planners, can also establish accurate default rules—in extreme cases, default rules that are tailored specifically to each member of the relevant population. On the basis of what choice architects know about you, they might well be able to identify exactly what you want—perhaps sooner, and perhaps even more accurately, than you yourself can. They can establish a Daily You, or a Monthly You, or a You This Year. They might do so by building on your own past choices. Or they might use other information—your age, your gender, your location, your health. They can relieve you of the obligation to choose, and decline to ask you questions, on the ground that they already know the answers.

Recall Pandora, the app that sets up a personalized radio station on the basis of your identification of a favorite singer or song. Pandora works because its mathematical algorithm accurately projects that if people like Song A, they will like Songs B, C, and D, too, because the latter songs are a lot like Song A. It is easy to imagine a movement toward Pandora everywhere (Pandorization?), with similar algorithms being used for a wide assortment of goods. If so, people might make a single choice, or a few, and the rest might happen automatically and by default, and people might like what they hear, see, and experience.

There is no question that the desire to make one's own decisions helps to define the human species. In many contexts, people want to exercise their choice-making muscles. People insist on active choosing, in part because they trust themselves more than others and in part because they want to use their autonomy and strengthen those muscles. Often they want to learn; many people are suspicious of default rules. But whether or not people notice them, such rules are omnipresent, and life could not be navigated without them. When people celebrate active choosing, it is often against a background set by defaults, which make choosing both manageable and feasible.

In Anglo-American political theory, it is standard to speak of "enabling constraints." The rules of grammar are one example; another is language itself. It is useless to deplore grammar or language, which make it possible to communicate even as, and because, they constrain. A constitution is itself an enabling constraint. Once a constitution is in place, people do not have to decide how many presidents to have, or whether there will be some kind of supreme court, or whether elections will be held.

In important respects, default rules make us free, if only because they allow us to have time for other matters. For private and public institutions, a central question is what happens if people do nothing, because nothing is exactly what people often do. If default rules are well chosen, they increase our welfare, because they make our lives go better. They also promote freedom, because they open up time for matters that are more pressing or important. Without default rules, it would be far more difficult for us to exercise our autonomy.

Much of my focus has been on the choice among three possibilities: impersonal default rules, active choosing, and personalized default rules. To decide which is best, we need to consider the costs of decisions and the costs of errors. That framework, rooted in welfarism, is not complete, but it captures much of the territory. To compress an extended argument, here are three sets of guidelines.

First: When the relevant group is not diverse, when people do not enjoy choosing, and when an impersonal default rule will satisfy the informed preferences of its members, it is generally most sensible to select that default rule rather than to require active choosing or to try to personalize. In such circumstances, an impersonal default rule will work well, in the sense that it will promote people's welfare. And if the underlying issue is complex and unfamiliar, active choosing might be a burden rather than a benefit. To that extent, the argument for use of a default rule is fortified. The principal qualification is that if learning and agency are important, there is a serious objection to the use of default rules of any kind.

Second: When the group is relevantly diverse, when choosing is actually preferred (perhaps because it is fun to choose), when learning and agency are important, or when private or public institutions cannot be trusted or lack good information about which default rule is best, active choosing has major advantages. If any of these conditions is met, there is an argument against an impersonal default rule and in favor of active choosing. When all of the conditions are met, that argument is overwhelming.

Third: When the group is relevantly diverse, when choosing is a burden rather than a benefit, and when personalized default rules are accurate, there is a strong argument for such rules. Because of human diversity, personalization can be a great boon; when choosing is an unwelcome burden, the case for active choosing is weakened. Personalized default rules have the potential to reduce the problems associated with one-size-fits-all defaults and thus to provide many of the benefits of active choosing, at least if the relevant choice architects are informed and trustworthy. If choice architects are reliable, there is always a good argument for personalized defaults, but that argument might be overcome when learning and agency matter—a recurring point in favor of active choosing.

In many domains, personalized default rules are the wave of the future. Inevitably, there will be a significant increase in personalization as greater information becomes available about the informed choices of diverse people. The coming wave is very much in progress. No one should doubt that it will create serious risks. I have emphasized the importance of privacy, learning, and self-development—and the need to insist on active choosing in many contexts. But there is reason for great optimism. Time is a precious commodity, perhaps the most precious of all, and we have more liberty, and more active choosing, if we end up with more of it. Sometimes the best choice is not to choose. Personalized default rules promise to make our lives not only simpler, healthier, and longer but also more free.

ACKNOWLEDGMENTS

My largest thanks are due to the late Edna Ullmann-Margalit for her work on closely related issues, for coauthoring several essays that helped to provide the foundations for this book, and for many relevant discussions. She was a truly remarkable philosopher, with a particular interest in presumptions and the limits of rationality and choice, and she was also a terrific friend and collaborator; this book would not have been possible without her.

I also owe particular thanks to Eric Johnson, who has done so much of the defining work on this subject, and who has been generous enough to discuss the underlying issues in some detail and to offer extensive comments on an early draft. Thanks in general to Richard Thaler, an amazing friend and coauthor; I have learned, and continue to learn, an immense amount from him. Our joint work, and our countless conversations, play a central role throughout this book. Thanks as well to Lucia Reisch for collaborative work that has greatly informed the discussion here, and for her valuable suggestions and comments on the basic argument. Riccardo Rebonato's superb book *Taking Liberties: A Critique of Libertarian Paternalism* (2012) helped to inspire and to inform many of the arguments presented in this book. I am most grateful to Rebonato for helpful discussions and comments.

Alex Flach, my editor, deserves particular thanks for general guidance and for detailed suggestions about the manuscript, which resulted in numerous improvements. I am grateful for his steady hand and sharp insights.

Thanks as well to Jon Elster, Elizabeth Emens, Craig Fox, Russell Korobkin, Jane Mansbridge, Yotam Margalit, Martha Nussbaum, Eric Posner, Tali Sharot, Larry Summers, David Tannenbaum, Adrian Vermeule, and Laura Willis for invaluable discussions and comments. Daniel Kanter, Lisa Marrone, Elsa Savourey, and Mary Schnoor provided excellent comments and valuable research assistance. Thanks also to my agent, Sarah Chalfant, for helpful guidance.

The book received its full development as the basis for the Quain Lectures at University College London, where they were delivered in October 2014. For countless valuable suggestions, I am most grateful to members of the audiences at the three lectures and the truly wonderful colloquium that followed them. Special thanks to George Letsas, my principal host, for extraordinary kindness and for superb comments and objections, which produced a number of improvements. During that whirlwind tour during the week of the Quain Lectures, I was privileged to present some of the argument at the London School of Economics and Politics; the Royal Society for the encouragement of Arts, Manufactures and Commerce; and Oxford University. Particular thanks to Tali Sharot, my host at the London School of Economics and Politics, for exceptional thoughts and suggestions.

Some of the argument here was also presented as the Edna Ullmann-Margalit Memorial Lecture at the Hebrew University of Jerusalem in May 2014. I was greatly honored to be asked to deliver that lecture and am thankful to my principal host, Maya Bar-Hillel, and all the Margalits, for their kindness and generosity.

Parts of the book have been delivered in many other places, including Cambridge University, the Copenhagen Business School, Dartmouth College, the National Science Foundation, the University of Pennsylvania Law School, and the British Academy, where early versions of some chapters were presented as the Maccabaean Lecture in Jurisprudence. For a host of suggestions, which significantly improved the manuscript, I am grateful to superb audiences at those lectures and to workshop participants at the University of California at Los Angeles, the University of Chicago Law School, and the J. F. Kennedy School of Government.

I am lucky indeed to have Harvard University as my academic home, and I thank Dean Martha Minow and President Drew Faust for making it such a congenial place in which to work. I spent much of the summer of 2014 at the Russell Sage Foundation in New York, and I thank Sheldon Danziger for making that extraordinary visit possible; I learned a great deal from the fellows there.

I have been working on default rules for at least twenty years. Most of that work appears in academic articles, and some of it can be found in three books: *Nudge: Improving Decisions about Health, Wealth, and Happiness* (2008) (written with Thaler), *Simpler: The Future of Government* (2013), and *Why Nudge? The Politics of Libertarian Paternalism* (2014). I have drawn from some of that work here, and for much of the discussion, I have drawn on earlier treatments of these topics in *Deciding by Default*, 162 U. PA. L. REV. 1 (2013) and *Choosing Not to Choose*, 64 DUKE L.J. 1 (2014); I am grateful to the editors of the University of Pennsylvania Law Review and the Duke Law Journal for permission to do so. For chapter 8, I have drawn from *Nudges vs. Shoves*, 127 HARV. L. REV. FORUM 210 (2014), and I am grateful as well to the editors of the *Harvard Law Review*.

INDEX